THE FOUNDATION OF PLOT

The Foundation of Plot

A Wait, Wait, Don't Query (Yet!) Book

ELENA HARTWELL

Elena Hartwell

ISBN: 979-8-9860206-0-0

First Printing, 2022

To the We Write Through writers workshop participants.
Seeing all of you on Zoom every Wednesday got me through lockdown.
I will be forever grateful for your time, attention, and good humor.
But even more, your friendship.
We are all in this together.

OTHER TITLES

Writing as Elena Hartwell

The Eddie Shoes mysteries

> *One Dead, Two to Go*
>
> *Two Heads are Deader Than One*
>
> *Three Strikes, You're Dead*

Writing as Elena Taylor

> *All We Buried*

CONTENTS

INTRODUCTION

> Attention to structure does not mean writing a formulaic manuscript. It means the creation of a strong foundation for whatever form a work takes.

After teaching writing for decades, I have a pretty good handle on what makes writers tick. Some writers embrace structure as a means to an end—a way to build a story from the outline up. Others write free-form, trusting the process to get them to a structured story … eventually.

Both of those processes can work, as does every method in between, because writers must find their own path. But regardless of process, ultimately—often after multiple drafts—a successful project relies on a strong foundation.

Understanding foundation will help writers improve their craft, but before going into that, let's talk about the application of the critical eye and the creative child. Wearing those hats—at the correct times—can aid writers with any project.

The critical eye is imperative, but not always at the beginning of a project. The critical eye helps to rewrite and shape and edit the work. It's how to cut much-loved material when it doesn't improve the manuscript or add to the plot. It's a way to analyze the art and apply the craft aspect of the writing process to produce a polished, query-ready manuscript.

The creative child, on the other hand, has little role during the final polish of a manuscript. That would be like a law student employing a five-year-old to take their bar exam. But the creative child is a great mode to work in at the beginning of a project and at various points along the way to explore without internal criticism or fear.

The creative child doesn't ask if anyone will like a manuscript. Or if it has value. Or if it's any good. The creative child lets the imagination run wild, dreaming up characters, scenarios, and descriptions of the setting. Or, in writing memoir or narrative nonfiction, the creative child plays with the memories or the resource material without limitations on which scenes or incidents to include, allowing the writer to build a more innovative manuscript.

At the start of the writing process, it can be helpful to let the creative child make big, bold choices. That boldness can get to the heart of the narrative. There's plenty of time later to engage the critical eye and finalize what should go in and what should stay out.

Building the foundation of a plot comes from a combination of the unhampered exploration of the creative child and the clinical precision of the critical eye. As writers, we can be playful with our creations, but we must also be merciless in cutting or rewriting what doesn't work.

In my work as a developmental editor, I often see writers stumble over structure in their works in progress. Sometimes an otherwise excellent manuscript—clear, concise language, an interesting premise, fascinating characters—fails because the material wanders or unfolds in a way that's less dramatic than it could be.

Whether a writer establishes their foundation in an outline or first draft or after several drafts doesn't matter; what does matter is eventually identifying and solidifying that foundation before starting to query.

The ideas in *The Foundation of Plot,* as well as the rest of the guidebooks in the Wait, Wait Don't Query (Yet!) series, can be used with short stories, novellas, novels, memoir, and narrative nonfiction. I often use the term "book" for ease of reading, but the theories in this guide apply to stories of any length. All stories—whether fictional or based on true events—have an underlying foundation. The better a writer understands that concept, the stronger the work can be.

There are outliers—successful books that defy the ideas in this guide. Some are much-loved books and best sellers. But consider both the evolution of books and the marketplace. There are bookcases full of wonderful, classic books that simply wouldn't be published today. They are too long, too wordy, and too full of tangents. Books—and other mediums for storytelling—evolve, whereas this guide focuses on the contemporary publishing industry.

The suggestions in this guide are also designed to help writers create the most *marketable* manuscript. A writer could ignore every suggestion in this guide and still write a polished, potentially compelling manuscript, but it might hurt that manuscript's chances for agent representation and publication with a legitimate publisher, or it might decrease the chances for solid reviews of a self-published book.

Lastly, use this guide as just that—a guide. Apply what resonates for any given work in progress and ignore what doesn't. But before sending queries to agents—or even drafts to beta readers—spend some time investigating plot foundation. Many concepts can be implemented before queries to agents or making the choice to self-publish.

So ... wait, wait, don't query yet—consider these concepts first.

Exercise 1: Letting Go of Perfection

It's often easier for a writer to tap into the critical eye than the creative child, but a writer is best served by the ability to shift between the two. To start out, let's get away from the critical voice that often impacts the ability to write messy drafts, which are an important part of the writing process. This exercise can be useful anytime, though it may come in especially handy when a writer feels blocked.

This is a five-minute timed writing. The goal is to write without engaging the critical eye. The goal here is *quantity*, not quality. This is a chance to explore character and/or plot without a sense of "having to get it right."

Step One: Set a timer for five minutes.

Step Two: Respond to either of the following prompts for five minutes. No matter what, don't stop writing. It's okay to go back and forth between the two prompts, but don't stop writing.

Prompt One: (Character Name) is driven by ...

Prompt Two: The most important event in the plot is when ...

Step Three: Once the timer sounds, go back and read the material—not for the quality, but for the *information*.

What new information came out about the character and/or plot? How did it feel writing this way? Was it fun? Scary? Boring? If it was fun, great! Stick with that feeling. The first draft should be fun; the creative child is on an adventure.

If it felt neutral or scary, it's likely the creative child doesn't feel safe. I would recommend doing this exercise until it feels better. It might be a way to start the writing routine every time. Quiet the critical eye and enjoy the process.

For those of us who find our way into the creative child easier than engaging the ability to self-edit, the exercise at the end of the next chapter will help writers activate the critical eye.

| 1 |

A Few Basics

> Raw doesn't mean terrible. It's just not ready for prime time.

Foundation—story structure—underlies everything that writers produce. No matter how avant-garde a literary work might appear on the surface, dig deep enough and a skeleton lies underneath.

Solidifying that underlying foundation can come at any point during the writing process. It could be in an outline before writing a single sentence, much as a carpenter uses a blueprint to build a house. Or it could be during a rough draft, determining the foundation through trial and error with character and action, like a dancer experimenting with choreography while the music plays.

What's important is that the process suits the writer for each individual project. For one project, a writer might benefit from building an outline first, while another project might evolve better with an organic method, discovering the foundation during a first draft.

There's no right or wrong about writing from an outline or relying on an organic process—only that the writer finishes that often stubborn first draft. Some writers mix and match, starting by writing organically, then creating an outline partway through, or changing the original outline completely as scenes begin to unfold. Or writers might

1

create a simple outline, then figure out the bulk of the project while building the scenes on the page.

It's never too late to make repairs. Even after multiple drafts, a writer can still improve a manuscript's foundation.

Regardless of when the writer pays attention to foundation, the manuscript will continue to evolve through each rewrite. From the first inklings of an idea to the final, polished manuscript, writers—whether they know it or not—shape and reshape the foundation of their work.

One concept that will be useful before going deeper into foundation is the difference between story and plot. Once that concept is clear, it may be easier to identify what does or doesn't work in a current project.

Story Versus Plot

As used in this guide, story is all-encompassing. It includes what happens before a book starts, everything in all the scenes, and every-thing that occurs off the page. It even includes what happens after the manuscript is finished, when the reader's imagination runs wild after "the end."

Plot, on the other hand, is made up solely of the events on the page.

One error writers make in their early—and sometimes even late—drafts is to include parts of the story that aren't necessary for the plot or leave out scenes a reader most needs on the page. This comes back to foundation. Those errors would be like using either too many joists to hold up a floor—making it heavy, cumbersome, and expensive—or not enough joists—causing the floor to fail the first time it bears weight.

In both of those instances, the writer has confused story and plot.

Falling in love with our own words, our characters, and the scenes that play out in our heads are constant dangers for writers. We want to include everything we research and invent. Sometimes this causes us to start too early in the lives of the characters and include scenes that are potentially beautifully written and explore behavior, motivation, and backstory but don't move the plot forward. We love our characters and believe a reader will be just as curious as we are about every aspect of their lives.

Readers, for the most part, want to follow a series of connected events leading to a satisfying conclusion. They don't want to read a series of unconnected events that send them in circles or down alleys that ultimately lead nowhere.

That is not the same as sending a reader down a wrong path for dramatic effect, as in a mystery where the detective follows the wrong lead. That experience can add to the plot, as a wrong lead can increase suspense. But it can be a problem if a detective goes down a wrong path and learns nothing from it.

Readers want each road the writer takes them down to add to the overall story—even when that road teaches the protagonist what they don't want or what won't solve the problem at hand.

A detective determining who *isn't* the culprit can be just as important—and satisfying in its own way—as when the detective catches the killer.

Readers may not be able to put this concept into words, but we've all heard comments like, "it took several chapters before I got into it" or "the writing was fine, but nothing happened at the beginning" or "I lost interest halfway through." Those are instances when a writer likely included material the reader didn't need—*no matter how good the quality of the writing.*

Don't confuse well-written sentences with a well-written book. High quality paints and canvases and excellent brushstrokes can still turn out an unsuccessful painting. A solid manuscript is more than just well-written sentences, beautifully crafted paragraphs, or even interesting chapters. A solid manuscript has a clear story arc, with each scene in each chapter adding to the whole and building a solid foundation.

The Heart of the Plot

The heart of the plot is constructed by characters, and characters are created primarily through action. Readers may love internal musings, descriptions, and snappy dialogue, but those details must combine with action to keep readers engaged. Further, as interesting as an active event might be, if it strays too far from the throughline of the plot, readers can lose interest.

Throughline, discussed in greater detail in Chapter Three, is the drive that pulls the characters and the readers through the story. It is the reason for everything the characters do and the impetus for readers to follow them.

Plot is built from characters in action driven by the throughline.

The Body of the Story

Story, on the other hand, includes all the other thoughts, actions, and experiences of the characters that *aren't* driven by the throughline. The events that don't relate to the drive of the narrative, such as sleeping, eating, doing laundry, or aimlessly driving around, happen in the lives of the characters but aren't part of the plot.

Even big, important events can be tangential to the throughline. No matter the importance of an event, if it does not relate to the throughline, it doesn't belong on the page.

Each action a character makes impacts themselves or other characters, who then react by performing another action, driving the throughline forward. Action, reaction, action. Over and over and over through the entire plot of a manuscript.

With memoir, the author took actions that impacted themselves or others, causing a reaction—just as with fictional characters. The author experienced additional events during the same time period as the events explored in the memoir, but if an event doesn't relate to the throughline, that event is story and doesn't belong in the plot.

For example, a memoir about surviving drug addiction wouldn't need to include a scene about going camping with friends if that scene does not relate *in any way* to surviving the drug addiction. No matter how active or well written that scene might be, it would be part of the author's story, not part of the memoir's plot, so it doesn't belong on the page.

Even if a plot unfolds slowly, such as a sweet romance that takes a long time before big actions take place, the characters still *do* things, based in part on emotions, to which other characters react. For example, the protagonist might dance around going on a date or fail to express interest in a potential partner. It's still action even when the characters fail to achieve their goals.

Story, on the other hand, isn't always built by actions. The body of the story includes inactive times, unrelated events, and actions of the character that are unrelated to the plot.

Plot is built from characters in action moving along a specific trajectory based on the drive of the throughline.

The Problem with Confusing Plot and Story

When a writer includes a lot of scenes that don't have action or have unrelated action, it can bog the material down, likely because the scenes are part of the body of the story, not the heart of the plot. At appropriate times, a character may turn introspective, and readers watch them think through a specific problem related to the throughline. But thinking on the page will only get a writer so far. Characters act, and those actions must be grounded in authentic emotions and the character's logic to pull them through the narrative.

It's true that some genres, such as thrillers, can be built with almost nonstop action. This genre might appear to lack emotion. But even thrillers have characters at the heart of events. The emotional state of the characters determines, in part, the actions they take. These actions must make sense—even if only in hindsight—due to who characters are and how they feel.

Lastly, if a character acts, creating an event, and then the next scene or chapter is unrelated to that event, readers can be left wondering, why did I need that action if nothing happened because of it? How is it that no one responded? Why am I reading about an unrelated event? The car chase was exciting, but what did it have to do with what came before and what occurred next?

If an event evokes those kinds of questions, and that event is never connected to the throughline, it's likely part of the story, not the plot, and it doesn't belong on the page.

The Impact of Multiple Point of View Characters and Omniscient Point of View

Point of view, or POV, determines the eyes through which a reader experiences the plot. Some manuscripts use multiple point of view characters and skip from one event with one character to a seemingly unrelated event with another, often chapter by chapter, but if a reader lays out all the chapters or scenes for each point of view character, that line of action, reaction, action will likely remain unbroken. The underlying foundation is harder to see because a different foundation exists underneath each plotline for each point of view character, but any material that is story, not plot, still doesn't belong on the page.

Omniscient point of view doesn't change that there is one set of eyes through which the reader experiences the plot. Omniscient POV provides an external, objective, distanced experience for the reader. While the omniscient POV (the narrator) can know the thoughts and experiences of all the characters, the reader sees those thoughts and experiences as filtered through that single omniscient perspective. Further, there will likely still be one single protagonist or main character.

It takes a keen hand to expertly weave multiple plotlines for multiple POV characters into one narrative or stay focused on a protagonist's plot when writing an omniscient POV, but a foundation underlies each thread, with a singular throughline underlying the entire manuscript.

Whether to write with a single POV character or multiple POV characters doesn't matter with regard to distinguishing story from plot; what matters is the execution of those threads and inclusion of only connected scenes in the manuscript.

Determining which events land on the page and which don't is one of the most important choices a writer can make. Even when telling a "true" story, such as with memoir or narrative nonfiction, most of the events authors or their subjects experienced in their lives won't make it on the page; otherwise, the manuscript would run thousands of pages. The trick is to show only the events that connect, one after the other, in a chain that leads the reader from beginning to end driven by the throughline.

For narrative nonfiction that follows multiple people, such as a sports team, a community, or a family unit, the common thread among them may be an issue or event that acts as the protagonist—for example, a sports team winning a season, a group making a large social shift such as a congregation welcoming female ministers, or a community coming to terms with a tragedy.

The Laramie Project, a play by Moisés Kaufman and members of the Tectonic Theater Project, has no specific protagonist. The entire community of Laramie, Wyoming, shares their reactions to the murder of Matthew Shepard in 1998. The murder is the throughline, the drive that connects all the individuals in the piece. Each scene relates to that specific event rather than a specific person. In this instance, scenes that don't relate in any way to Matthew Shepard or his murder would be story, not plot.

Keeping in mind the difference between story and plot, let's investigate the most basic form of plot foundation.

Three Integral Parts of the Plot: Basic Foundation

This basic foundation always appears during a finished first draft. For outliners, the basic foundation appears in the outline. Regardless of how writers achieve their first drafts, through outlining then writing or writing organically, the principles of the three integral parts of a plot apply equally. Even though the plot may change extensively through rewrites, the first draft contains three integral parts—a beginning, a middle, and an end—without which it's not a first draft; it's only a first draft in progress.

Once those three sections are in place, no matter how poorly written, it's a perfect *first* draft. It's not polished. It's not submission ready. But that's not the role of the first draft. The *only* role of the first draft is the construction of a beginning, a middle, and an end.

- A beginning gets the story going.
- A middle includes action rising to a climax.
- An end brings the plot to a conclusion.

Easy, right?

A basic foundation is simple, not easy. Simple because the three parts are identifiable. But not easy. It takes a lot of work to create the scenes that make up those three parts.

Writers often struggle with allowing themselves to write badly. But a first draft won't be polished. A first draft will have holes and plot points that don't fit together and characters behaving in ways that don't make sense, not to mention grammatical errors and typos and all the additional polishing details that won't matter until several drafts down the road.

One concept that can help writers build a first draft of a manuscript or first draft of an outline is to keep in mind that perfection is not the goal.

Perfecting the writing in the first draft might, in fact, cause the writer to fail before leaving the starting gate. Energy spent on polishing a first draft can waste the writer's time and end in frustration because it's impossible to polish unfinished material. A writer's time is better spent focusing on the goals of building a beginning, a middle, and an end than to clean up language and grammatical errors in an unfinished first draft.

For those writers who struggle with continually polishing early chapters rather than moving forward and writing to the end, use the exercise in the introduction to engage the creative child until that exercise becomes easy. Let the creative child move forward without fear or concern for perfection. Like a feral horse racing across the prairie, let the creative child write unfettered and sort out what does or doesn't work later. As author Jodi Picoult famously said, "You can't edit a blank page."

Another common problem I encounter with writers is the inability to finish a first draft because they write like gangbusters for fifty pages, then fizzle out. These writers likely tap into their creative child easily, finding that fun rush of adrenaline as the words pour out. But the writing comes to an abrupt halt when the process gets hard.

While this next exercise is for everyone to do, it may be especially useful for those who need to learn how to force themselves to finish a scene or a draft. The critical eye is for more than editing. It's also the taskmaster when writing becomes a challenge.

Exercise 2: Engaging the Critical Eye

Engaging the critical eye is more than just checking for typos and grammatical errors. Engaging the critical eye can also help writers cut material they love or acknowledge when a scene doesn't work. Most importantly in the early stages, the critical eye can help writers get from point A to point Z. That's because the critical eye is the heavy lifter—the one who digs in when writing gets hard.

Stuck trying to finish a first draft? It can help to write scenes for the beginning, the middle, and the end without trying to make them perfect.

This may feel impossible because the writer doesn't know what the book is truly about. But here's what is so beautiful about writing. It doesn't matter if scenes are right or wrong. Nothing is final until a book is published.

It may feel like the creative child should be tapped here, but if the creative child was able to work, the writer wouldn't be stuck.

Just like a child might want to eat ice cream all the time or never go to bed, the creative child likes to write when it's fun. Sometimes the grown-up in the writing process, the critical eye, needs to step in and get the draft finished.

To tap into that aspect of the critical eye, the following exercise can help, no matter how far along a writer is in the current work in progress.

Use the critical eye to force three scenes. Don't worry about how well they are written. Just make sure they get done. Be aware of the fact that the writing is stalled. That's the other role of the critical eye: to help the writer keep moving, even when they think they can't.

For writers with a full draft, try the exercise anyway and see if the result fits with the current draft or introduces something unexpected that could be incorporated into the work in progress. For anyone starting a brand-new project, this exercise will help form the foundation.

Step One: Write three sentences by filling in the parentheticals with names and actions from your work in progress.

1: The plot starts when character (name) does (action).

2. Things get really interesting when (same character) does (action).

3. Things are resolved when (same character) is finally able to (action).

Use this information as a guide to keep the plot moving forward. These sentences are the basis for three scenes to help build the beginning, the middle, and the end.

Step Two: Use the first sentence to write a scene for the opening.

Step Three: Use sentence two to write a scene for the potential climax.

Step Four: Use sentence three to write a scene for the ending.

Step Five: For those with an existing manuscript, use the new scenes to bridge missing sections or start a new series of events. For those that are stuck, use the scenes generated by this exercise to help build the manuscript through to the end. For those starting a new project, these scenes can act as anchors for a full first draft.

With that exercise completed, let's take a closer look at the three basic parts of plot.

| 2 |

The Beginning

> If a writer can't hook a reader at the beginning, it doesn't matter how great the rest of the book might be—no one will ever read it.

As Lewis Carroll wrote in *Alice in Wonderland*, "Begin at the beginning … and go on till you come to the end: then stop."

Easier said than done.

A popular piece of advice bandied about at writing workshops and conferences is to start as late as possible in a story and get out as early as possible.

That may be true, but it's not useful advice if a writer doesn't know how that translates to the page. To get a better understanding of that concept, let's look at the function of a beginning. Understanding the function of the beginning can help determine the best place to start.

The beginning of a manuscript carries a lot of responsibility. The writer and the reader seal their pact early on. This means the reader has an expectation of what kind of book the author wrote: how realistic, how violent, how profane, how funny. If it conforms to genre conventions or not. Whether it will unfold fast or slow. While writers can vary the pace of the scenes or surprise a reader with unconventional genre choices, authors should be cautious about changing rules mid-stream as this can turn readers off and cause them to stop reading.

In addition to building a pact with the reader, the beginning of a manuscript usually contains a hook to get readers' attention from the very beginning. The hook can be set with a variety of techniques such as an enticing first line, dropping readers into action, and heightened language.

Engage the Reader—the Hook

Readers have millions of titles to choose from when they determine what book to read next. And readers choose titles in a myriad of ways: recommendations by friends or reviewers, author recognition, or topic. Sometimes the choice is random. A reader walks into a bookstore—or clicks around online—looking at a specific category of book. They like a cover, so they read the title. They like the title, so they read the book description. They like the description, so they read the first page.

That's often all the time a writer is given to convince a reader to carry the book to the cashier or click the buy button.

One page.

The writer must engage the reader from the very first paragraph, and a hook can help do that.

An Enticing First Line

The perfect, engaging first line can get people to read the first paragraph.

Consider this line: "Call me Ishmael." Melville's famous first sentence sets up the narrator of his epic work *Moby Dick*. Part of the genius with this opening is its simplicity, but the line also serves a lot of purposes with just three words. It shows us who the storyteller is—Ishmael. It shows the voice of the novel—Ishmael's. It shows that he's settling in to spin a yarn, speaking directly to the reader. The unusual name entices us to read further.

Look back through favorite books. What opening lines work best? There's a reason why the opening line to *Rebecca* by Daphne du Maurier is so often quoted. Dickens's "It was the best of times, it was the worst of times," is even more famous than the book itself—more people recognize those words than know the title of the book is *A Tale of Two Cities*. Great opening lines build suspense, compelling readers to find out what's next.

Dropping Readers into Action

Another effective way to hook a reader is to start with the characters smack in the middle of action.

If we were to write a novel through the course of this guide, here are two potential ways to start:

Candice walked to the toaster and pulled two slices of wheat bread out of the bag that sat on the counter. She dropped them in and pushed the lever before crossing to the coffee pot. Scooping the grounds into the filter, she looked out the window at the river in the distance. She could glimpse the top of the bridge a few miles away through the trees.

Consider this alternative:

Balanced on the railing, Candice stared into the rushing water below. The drop might not kill her, but the fact that she couldn't swim would soon render the issue moot.

The second example starts much later in Candice's day. She's had her toast and coffee, traveled the short distance to the river, and is now poised to commit suicide. The choice to start the plot at that specific moment works as a hook, whereas the first example—where Candice makes toast—might hold a reader's interest to read further, but not because of the immediate action of the character. Making toast and looking out the window isn't very dynamic.

Heightened Language

Heightened language can also function as a hook. The opening paragraph of any literary work by authors such as Jamie Ford or Toni Morrison will captivate the reader through its language. The hook is the author's use of words. Look at the difference between these sentences:

Balanced on the railing, Candice stared into the rushing water below. The drop might not kill her, but the fact that she couldn't swim would soon render the issue moot.

Or

Land. Bridge. Sky. Candice balanced on her toes. Beneath her, water raced from mountain to sea, with no sympathy for her plight. Should she fall, the splash meant no more than a branch escaping its tree.

The first example uses more casual language and sentence structure. The second example uses fragments and less conventional sentence structure along with less common word choices. They both describe the same thing—Candice, balanced on a rail, poised to jump.

This use of heightened language is similar—but not the same—as a clear author's voice. Authors who are not "literary" per se can still have clear, authentic, engaging voices. Language doesn't have to be heightened or poetic to pull a reader in. Stephen King is not considered a literary author, yet his voice is clear, recognizable, and engaging—so engaging he has millions of readers around the globe.

After hooking the reader, the beginning has more heavy lifting to do. The beginning also sets up character, location, events, genre, world-building, and author voice. Each of these can also hook the reader if they appear in the opening pages.

Character as Hook and Beyond

Engaging characters can serve double duty, acting as both a hook and as part of the larger role of the beginning.

One of the most successful ways to hook readers is to give them a character with a clear objective, a big obstacle, and a sense of the stakes. Objectives, obstacles, and stakes will be topics in another book in this series, *The Construction of Character*, but for now, think of it this way: readers connect with characters who want something. This includes the author in memoir and the real people in narrative nonfiction. Even "real" characters have goals.

Readers often hope a character will achieve a goal because readers relate to wanting something—*even if the character wants something very different than the reader does*. It's having a goal that makes the character relatable, not the goal itself.

Returning to our example of Candice, let's take a closer look at what she might be struggling with. She isn't struggling with whether to jump; she is struggling with how to stop her pain. To make her character act as a hook, we could show her internal conflict at the very beginning of the manuscript:

Candice balanced on the edge. She'd been alone too long, and the pain of her isolation overshadowed everything else. All she had to do was let go.

The sound of barking pulled her from the hypnotic action of the rapids. The swirl of the fast-moving river held a dog captive, spinning him helplessly in the water's grasp. Hopping from her perch on the rail, Candice stumbled down the steep embankment. Shoving sadness aside, she made her way to the dog—jammed now against the concrete bulwark of the bridge by the power of the current. Wading out chest-deep, she grabbed hold of the panicked animal and began to work her way back to shore.

In just two paragraphs, two clear and distinct objectives emerge for this character. We start out with the understanding that she's in emotional pain and looking for a way to change that, with suicide as an option. With the arrival of the dog, her objective shifts to saving the animal. We pull for her to save the dog, in part because there is the potential for her to solve her feelings of isolation.

Save the dog, save herself.

Readers invest in Candice because she wants something that has obstacles and stakes. She has an immediate objective—save the dog—and an overarching objective—stop her own pain.

Setting up Characters

Beyond acting as a hook, opening chapters introduce readers to characters who will matter for the duration of the manuscript. Even if the protagonist doesn't appear in the first chapter, they typically appear near the beginning. In our example with Candice, readers can guess that both Candice and the dog are going to be pivotal characters. It may be that the dog isn't going to be central, but perhaps the owner of the dog will be. Or at least the event with the dog will send Candice into a new direction and away from taking her own life.

Notice the action here will likely set up a question in the reader's mind. Readers looking for answers will keep reading to find out what she is going to do next. Will she get what she wants? What else will happen in this place? If the questions are interesting and the answers feel important, readers won't put the book down. And neither will agents or editors during the query process.

One of the most important aspects of setting up characters is to determine the point of view character and the protagonist, and whether they are the same.

Point of View Character Versus Protagonist

Readers want to know whose point of view they will follow through the plot and who is the protagonist. Point of view, as discussed earlier, determines the eyes through which a reader experiences the plot, whereas the protagonist is the main character.

Let's take a closer look at those two terms—protagonist and point of view character—as they interact closely with foundation, and while these are often the same in contemporary storytelling, there are instances when the primary POV character is not the main character. For example, Nick tells the story of Jay Gatsby in *The Great Gatsby*, and Ishmael tells the story of Captain Ahab in *Moby Dick*.

Unless a writer is working in literary fiction, or narrative nonfiction where the author relays a real-life story they observed or researched, it's often the stronger choice to keep the primary POV character and pro- tagonist the same. Memoir is written by the author about the author, so the author is the protagonist and the point of view character.

An obvious complication to having the POV character and the protagonist the same character is when a writer has multiple point of view characters who are equal in importance. For example, a romance novel may have point of view chapters from both partners, so both POV characters are the protagonists.

In contrast, a mystery may present most chapters in the detective's point of view and a few scattered chapters written from the killer's point of view. Even during the killer's point of view chapters, the detective remains the protagonist, as it's the detective's story that read- ers follow.

Some carefully constructed multiple POV novels have more than one protagonist. *Gone Girl* by Gillian Flynn successfully weaves two main characters together. And George R.R. Martin uses a host of main characters for each of his Game of Thrones books—but those kinds of projects are difficult.

For the most part, readers like to know who to root for, or at least, who to engage with. Look for more on point of view and protagonists in *The Construction of Character*, but keep in mind that establishing the POV and protagonist, whether singular, separate, or multiple, occurs in the beginning of a manuscript.

Major Players

Readers also like to meet at least some of the major players early on. This does not mean an important character can't show up at the end, but at least a few of the most important characters appear at the beginning.

The beginning can be a place to identify the helpers as well as the individuals who create issues for the protagonist. An enemy or a stalwart companion can fill out a manuscript's beginning section.

Writers may lead readers to believe that some characters are friends only to reveal later that they aren't, or introduce foes who ultimately become friends, but one important aspect in the beginning is that the writer establishes at least some of the important relationships and reveals the starting dynamic between the protagonist and these other characters.

Location

Location is an important component at the beginning of a manu-script—readers want to know where they are in time and space, and setting can also make for a surprisingly good hook.

Readers take great pleasure in "traveling" as they read, visiting places they know and love and places they have never been before. Creating a dynamic sense of place can hook a reader's attention because they want to see more and discover the characters who will fill those spaces.

Readers enjoy details about the locations in which a story exists. I use story here rather than plot because readers will imagine the places and events that occur off the page, what happened before, and what happens after "the end."

Location can also serve to heighten the tension in a situation. The environment can work against the characters and add to the danger. The heavy current Candice fights could function as a metaphor for her emotional battle. Or, as danger can also be psychological or emotional, the appearance of a dog in physical danger can heighten Candice's emotional danger.

Location could also provide an anchor for the characters, function-ing as a safety net. In *The Hobbit*, the Shire protects Bilbo Baggins, which is one of the reasons leaving is scary, making for a big obstacle and increasing the stakes when he is confronted with the possibility of the journey. If the Shire wasn't safe, Bilbo would have less of a reason to remain at home.

When a location is a real-world place, readers want details they could experience themselves, and potentially already have. If a location is pure fantasy, readers likely need more information from the writer to picture all the locations in the story. It's okay if every reader imagines something different, but if a world is well-described, if discussed, readers can understand how each arrived at their own version.

Few experiences are worse for a reader than imagining a location for a story, making decisions in the dark because the writer hasn't added much, only to have a writer describe it in greater detail late in the plot, forcing the reader to throw out initial ideas about location and start over again with the new information. That can be disorienting and could make a reader stop reading.

A few specific details can provide a lot more for a reader than long but vague descriptions. Even when the same number of words is used, specific choices can make a world of difference. Consider the following for the world we are building for Candice:

The bridge was long and narrow and crossed a busy river that ran between a lake and the ocean several miles away.

Versus:

The concrete and steel bridge once carried trains across the Weymouth River, but now only foot traffic crossed the rapids below.

With almost the same number of words, one description is vague and provides few specifics. The second shows the materials the bridge is built with, the name of the river, and the fact the old railroad bridge now carries pedestrians, not trains.

That's a lot more specific information, allowing readers to imagine it for themselves and not have to go back later and change the images with the addition of new information. In the first example, the bridge could be wood, concrete, steel—there's no way to know. It could be a car bridge, a foot bridge, even a suspension bridge, and a "busy" river could indicate a lot of boat travel or fast-moving rapids.

The specificity of description and location helps the reader build an accurate picture.

Description of location can function like a hook, making readers wonder what else they will learn about where the story takes place. It also sets the tone for how characters interact with and feel about their location.

Events

Plots consist of interconnected events. A writer may include events at the beginning that don't immediately relate directly to the plot, building the world of the character or showing what they have at stake, but at a minimum those events will resonate later in the narrative. For example, readers might be shown what the character will have to lose at a later critical point, where the reader will have an "ah ha, that's why that was important" realization.

But a very specific event does occur near the beginning that launches the protagonist into a new direction. That event is often called the inciting incident.

Though I'll go into this deeper in Chapter Five with the definition of common terms, think of the inciting incident this way: a singular event intrudes into the established life of the protagonist and launches the plot. The hook captures a reader's attention, and the inciting incident sends the protagonist on a journey.

Consider our event with Candice. It would be possible to begin with her at home alone and lonely, showing readers her isolation before she finds the dog. That's a valid place to start. She gets up and does her routine, making toast and drinking coffee, all the while considering jumping from the bridge. That scene could develop her character, even though those events aren't immediately related to finding the dog. But her life is clearly changed when she comes home with the dog, filling the otherwise empty house with sound and movement and company—a juxtaposition of context from the opening scenes.

But it's also dynamic to have her start at the bridge contemplating suicide and the dog shows up immediately. Through well-crafted exposition, we can always show the reader in later scenes how lonely and isolated she felt before the dog came into her life. Either way would work, so we're going to decide based on the kind of book we're writing. If the book is going to be in the suspense genre, we'd likely start with action. If we want to write women's fiction and we plan to delve into her psyche and relationships and work life, we might choose to start with her at home, showing readers more of her current situation and letting events unfold at a slower pace.

Certain genres—thrillers, for example—require more action up front, whereas other genres, such as sci-fi and fantasy, allow for more world-building.

Regardless, readers want to know what happens next. And—based on the genres they typically read—they have expectations about how those events will transpire.

Readers want to know how the primary character will react to each event. The incident of the dog in the river shows readers a lot about Candice. But what she does with the dog after she gets him out of the water establishes her character even more. She could set him loose, expecting him to find his own way home. She could take him home to dry him off and make sure he's not a stray. The connection between her reaction (the dog needs help), action (she saves the dog), reaction (what she does with the dog next) moves the plot forward.

Readers want to know the next logical step, not spend time with a random, disconnected event, no matter how well written that event might be.

If we went from Candice finding the dog to a scene about her going to the market and running into an ex and his new wife, we could absolutely establish her loneliness, but readers would be shouting at us (and Candice) … but what happened with the dog?

Genre Conventions

The beginning establishes genre. Genre is more than just a category on a bookstore shelf. Genre is a shorthand way for readers to know if the book falls into a category they read. It's also a shorthand way for agents to know if they can successfully represent a manuscript. Agents sell books to editors they have built a relationship with, typically within the genres they most often represent. An agent might love a book, but if they have no relationships with editors of that genre, they may find it difficult to place that book with a publisher.

I like to explain genre in the context of a restaurant. Think about all the types of restaurants in the world. If someone is a vegan, they won't look forward to going to a barbecue joint. It doesn't matter if it's the best in the state; they are not going to enjoy it. Pulled pork and baked beans cooked with bacon will not serve as a vegan meal.

Similarly, if readers don't want violence on the page, they are not going to enjoy a violent thriller, no matter how well it's written or what awards it wins. If a reader isn't interested in love stories, romance novels are never going to make the list of what to read next. Writers sometimes make the mistake of thinking everyone needs to love their work, but that's neither possible nor practical.

A better goal is to want all the people who read a specific genre to love their work. That's the important demographic.

Writers should read in their genre and know their genre.

If a writer isn't sure what genre their work fits into, they would be smart to keep writing and reading until they do. It's virtually impossible to pitch a manuscript to an agent without identifying the genre. Let's compare that to internet dating.

Consider the following if it came from strangers online through a dating site:

Date #1: I'm not going to tell you where we are going or what we are going to do, so you don't know what to wear or what to expect, but I know you're going to love it.

Date #2: I see that you love pizza and walking on the beach. Let's meet at the beach. I'll bring a pizza with any toppings you like along with your beverage of choice, and then we can take a walk along the sand.

Which date is more appealing? Okay, so the second one might be creepy too, but at least it's clear about what to expect.

Writers employ many ways to show genre from the very first paragraph. Dark atmosphere for suspense. A crime scene for a mystery. A chance meeting for romance. Whether it's heightened language for a literary work or a description of a spaceship or futuristic lab for science fiction, it's important to understand how plots in a given genre start out in other published, contemporary books of the same genre. Identify what gets included and what gets left out.

Writers don't need to build something completely new—readers love familiarity. They want characters to be unique and the plot to be surprising, but they also want to know the pact between writer and reader will be honored. That means a sweet romance won't turn into a horror novel halfway through, with the lovers brutally murdered in a swamp. A cold war thriller won't turn into a slow-moving, coming of age story about a kid with special needs. The reader wants to know what they signed up for—and more importantly, what they paid for.

Writers don't have to know exactly what genre their work will fall into while drafting the manuscript, but choices made during each draft will lead the author down the genre/category road. And long before querying a manuscript, the writer should know their genre and even subgenre where appropriate.

Knowing the genre or category from the beginning can be useful because conventions exist within each genre, and these can be mined from the first draft. Writers should consider conventions and expectations for different age ranges if a manuscript is not for adult readers. The more a writer reads in their genre and/or age category, the better. For example, profanity in middle grade stories is rare, but we do see profanity in young adult novels. In fact, it is becoming more and more expected.

A manuscript is art when it sits on the writer's computer, but the minute a writer starts to query, that same manuscript becomes a product. Products have requirements, and even though writers can bend or break the rules, each time they do, the number of agents willing to look at that manuscript gets smaller.

A cross-genre manuscript can be very successful. Some amazing books cross genre lines, but that can also make selling a manuscript harder, and writers must understand all the genres combined in their work.

World-Building

The beginning establishes the world of the manuscript to varying degrees. While world-building is important in any manuscript, some genres benefit from extra attention. Science fiction, fantasy, and historical all lend themselves to greater world-building details. When readers are unable to directly experience the world where the story takes place, strong descriptions make for a more satisfying read.

World-building differs from location in a variety of ways. Think of location as providing the specific "where" of the story, such as a house or a neighborhood or a city, while world-building provides the totality of that location—everything from culture and demographics to wildlife, weather, and technological advancement.

When world-building, writers should utilize all the senses. It's important to add not just what the characters see, but also what they can hear, touch, taste, and smell.

If we were to world-build for Candice's plot, we could include many details in this opening. Where in the country does this take place? If this bridge is in a gritty, urban setting, that's much different than if it's in a rural area with no one else around. If this is contemporary—happening today—that's different than if we set this story a hundred years ago. These are the kinds of details we want to establish at the beginning to orient the reader and place them inside Candice's world.

For Candice, we could start with the same plot but include different world-building.

Candice balanced on the metal railing at the side of the railroad bridge. Off to her left, amidst the miles of trains and tracks, engines chuffed out their diesel breaths, while men in bright orange safety jackets became exotic insects from so far away. Below her, the murky waters of the river were slick with oil, sparkling with the rainbow hue of manmade poisons.

Here's an alternative:

Candice balanced on the ancient wooden railing of the footbridge over the river. Off to her left, she could see over the tops of the willows into MacIntyre's orchard, where she'd done her share of stealing apples as a child. The trees were bare now at the end of winter but would soon bud with the coming of spring.

Candice does the same thing in both examples. She stands on top the railing of a bridge and contemplates jumping. But the world-building is completely different, changing the tone and feel of the manuscript. Both are valid, but the choice of world-building will have major repercussions on the final product—including genre.

Author Voice

One of the most important aspects of the beginning of a manuscript is to establish author voice. A strong voice is often the best way to hook an agent. It's also very hard to define. Think of author voice like that of an artist's style. It doesn't take a degree in art to recognize a painting by Picasso versus Georgia O'Keeffe. Similarly, it's not hard to pick up a novel by Zora Neale Hurston or Amy Tan and recognize their voices.

Author voices develop over time. Just as Picasso didn't start out a cubist, earlier works by even the most recognizable of authors can sound very different compared to later years.

Every choice a writer makes connects to their author voice: word choice, character actions, genre, issues and themes, a conversational or formal tone. Whatever makes a writer unique shines through the work. Continue to notice personal language use, choice of characters, situations, and other decisions unconsciously made while writing and rewriting. The more a writer writes, the clearer their voice becomes.

The beginning of a story, whether fiction, memoir, or narrative nonfiction, has a specific role to play. It provides an immediate hook, introduces characters, determines the POV character (and protagonist if they are different), describes location, includes events, clarifies genre, and establishes world-building, all while showing off the author voice.

That's a lot of work for one section. But the stronger the beginning, the more engaged the reader will be. Manuscripts need a strong foundation to hold up the middle, which is the longest and most challenging section to write.

Exercise 3: Assess the Beginning of a Work in Progress or Start to Build a New Project

With a work in progress, identify each item on the following list. Determine if each of these items is clear in the beginning. If not, where does the beginning fail, and how can that current failure be successfully rewritten?

To start a new project, describe each of the following with at least one paragraph. Not all of these will happen on the first page or even the first chapter, but they will occur near the beginning and include the event that launches the rest of the book. This would be a time to go back to Exercise 2 and review the first sentence and the scene generated from that sentence.

The List:

Hook: What happens on the first page that will make readers keep reading?

Characters: Who do readers meet in the opening chapters? Why would readers want to engage with them?

Point of View and Protagonist: Whose eyes do readers see through? Is this the same as the main character? If not, who is the main character, and why are we seeing them through another character's eyes?

Location: Is the location clearly established? What are the primary characteristics?

Events: Is there action in the opening?

Inciting Incident: What specific event prompts the rest of the manuscript?

Genre: What genre or genres does the manuscript fit into?

World-Building: How well developed is the world of the manuscript?

Analyzing the answers to each of these will illuminate sections that need work or invent enough information to write a solid opening. If there is no answer for some of these, mark that item and refer to it later, as future exercises and additional writing will likely generate a response that can then be applied to the manuscript.

| 3 |

The Middle

Dear Reader, Now that I have you, how do I keep you?

The beginning hooks the reader, but the middle must keep them. The three worst letters a writer can spot in a review today are DNF. To have a reader post "did not finish" is devastating. Yes, it's true that person bought the book, checked it out of the library, or borrowed it from a friend, but they didn't like it enough to finish it. Even worse, they are telling other people that they didn't finish it. Further, if a reader doesn't finish a book on platforms like Kindle Unlimited, the author earns less, receiving payment only for the electronic pages read.

Too many DNFs showing up on Goodreads can also cost a writer future readers. It can impact the sales and success of the *next* book, including the likelihood a traditional publisher will offer a contract.

But most importantly, writers want to produce the best book possible, and that means a successful middle.

The middle is the longest section of a plot. It's where the bulk of the events and character development happen. It's where the stakes rise the highest, the objectives become the clearest, and the obstacles grow in importance. Regardless of genre or category, events become more interesting and important as the reader progresses, until the plot reaches the highest point. Then the middle ends with the climax, which also begins the ending.

Events

The middle is composed of a series of events linked by the actions and reactions of characters.

Plot, as discussed earlier, is made up of events on the page. Each event links to the one before and the one after. Even if the connection between events isn't immediately clear to the reader, the writer knows exactly how those events connect, and the reader will understand that connection by the end of the plot.

Though this process can be complicated by multiple point of view characters—discussed further in the book *The Construction of Character*—even an omniscient or multiple POV manuscript is still constructed with events connected to other events, and those connections will be revealed by the end of the manuscript.

Not only is a plot made up of events connected to each other, but the events also impact each other. For example, a detective finds a clue and then acts on that clue. The scene where the detective finds the clue relates directly to the scene where the detective acts on it. Perhaps a fingerprint identifies a suspect, which then leads to an interview with that suspect.

If a detective finds a clue, then goes home and has pizza and watches television, those two scenes are not connected other than through chronology. If nothing in the scene with the detective eating pizza and watching television relates to solving the mystery, even if it is chronologically sequential, that scene is story, not plot. They are connected in time, but one does not impact the other.

Manuscripts often come to me for developmental editing filled with great scenes, well-written events, and interesting characters, along with tight writing, good descriptions, and genre-appropriate content. That may sound fine, but if the scenes are not prompted by earlier scenes or don't prompt any scene that comes after, it's a foundational problem. If a scene does not relate to what motivates the character—or the author in the case of memoir—the scene lacks drive. Those scenes, no matter how well written, do not belong on the page.

A scene might not connect immediately but should connect eventually.

One way to understand the relationship between events is with the concepts of throughline, spine, or big question, each of which combine events with drive.

Events are the actions a character takes. Drive is the impetus pushing a character through the plot—their motivation or super-objective—which helps determine their actions.

The throughline, spine, or big question are three different ways to understand how events combine with drive to underpin each scene in a manuscript.

These terms are related but provide three different ways to think about the concept. All three can be applied at any point in the drafting process.

Throughline

The throughline sends the protagonist along the narrative arc, like an unbroken path through the wilderness. The trees and bushes alongside are scenes that occur off the page. The path is made up of events that occur on the page, joined together with objectives.

Protagonists want something in every moment of every scene throughout a manuscript. Those wants are called objectives. Specific objectives cause characters to act in certain ways; these actions prompt events, which then impact the world they live in, to which other characters then react. It's cause and effect. Each event is followed by another event, prompted by the action of a character. Drive plus event equals throughline.

An objective combined with an action to move a character toward that objective builds the path. Objectives, obstacles, and stakes, discussed in depth in the book *The Construction of Character*, are only one aspect of the throughline. Objectives, obstacles, and stakes, without action, are not a throughline. A throughline requires action.

Protagonists can't just want something. They also actively pursue that goal. Readers aren't engaged by scenes where a protagonist does nothing except wish their life was different. Readers engage when characters reach for goals, even if the goal is to flee from their heart's desire or if the character fails in spectacular fashion for the bulk of the plot. Readers want to see characters fail and pick themselves up and try again.

This desire to see people in action allows for characters to make bad choices, run from what they want and fear, and generally not do what they should until the climax of the manuscript, because even when failing, they are, in fact, moving toward their long-term goals.

The throughline flows from the single largest driver of the protagonist, their super-objective—the big goal that is the reason for the book. The throughline is the path they take to pursue what their heart desires most. If they get it and it's good, happy ending. If they get it and it's bad, tragic ending. If they don't get it but they get something else that's better, happy ending. If they get it and it's fine, but they realize it's not what they want or need, that's a poignant or bittersweet ending.

Much of writing a solid manuscript comes down to understanding what a character wants. Smaller goals can change from scene to scene, but the largest want, the ultimate goal—the super-objective—remains the same from beginning to end.

In *The Hobbit*, Bilbo Baggins wants to know if he can survive an adventure and return home. That goal is his super-objective. He fights it at the start, but deep in his heart, it's what he wants more than anything else. He proves that with his decision to go, which he does near the beginning of the novel. His super-objective is even made clear in the subtitle: *The Hobbit, or There and Back Again.*

From the moment he's presented with the idea of a journey, his desire prompts every event that takes him to the Lonely Mountain, followed by a much less detailed, but no less important, trip back to the Shire. Each event links to the one before and pushes him toward his ultimate goal—not just going on an adventure but returning safely home. If the return home weren't part of his super-objective, the book could end when Bilbo and the Dwarves successfully defeat the dragon Smaug. Events, driven by a super-objective equals the throughline.

Another way to think about this concept of events plus motivation is the spine.

Spine

Rather than visualizing a path through the woods, visualize the spine as the part of the skeleton on which each scene relies. To stand, the bones must attach to each other. The spine is a central line connecting each scene. Events are like bones, joined by tendons built by motivation.

Imagine each specific event is a vertebra. Each event connects to the next with tendons. Tendons are objectives. With any missing bone, the skeleton will fall. If any tendon sags or is missing, the next event can't occur. Events and objectives combine like bones and tendons to hold the plot together.

The other parts of the skeleton, arms and legs and fingers, are the events that happen off the page; they are part of the story, but not part of the plot. Like the dorsal fin of a whale arcing out of the water, the plot shows only the backbone, but the rest of the animal exists, unseen under the water, holding the plot aloft.

The spine of *The Hobbit* is the journey. Each scene is about the journey Bilbo takes. From the moment he leaves the Shire to the moment he returns, everything focuses on the journey.

Some writers find it easier to imagine events as steps along a path, while others might prefer to picture a spine holding up the skeleton of plot. Any missing chunk will keep the skeleton from standing upright.

The Big Question

A third way to think about this concept of events plus motivation is the big question.

Manuscripts ask a big question at the beginning, which is then answered at the end. The question pulls the reader through the manuscript. The big question for *The Hobbit* could come directly from the subtitle: *There and Back Again.* The big question for *The Hobbit* could be phrased, does Bilbo make it there and back again?

Every event moves the reader toward the answer to that question. Every event is driven by a motivation or a goal. Motivation plus event equals the answer.

Let's return to the story of Candice and the dog. A number of possible throughlines, spines, or big questions exist for her story. I've picked one to demonstrate how to view it through these three different lenses.

Candice's Throughline

We could think of Candice's throughline as her need to find community. Perhaps her goal is to build a circle of people who make her feel like she belongs.

We could imagine her throughline this way: Candice searches for community.

Every scene we write will connect to her primary goal, including scenes where she's shut out or can't connect with others as she tries but fails to achieve her super-objective.

Keep in mind, the character may not be aware of her super-objective, which is the motivation prompting the events in the throughline, but as authors, we are aware the entire time, quietly manipulating the character's actions because we know what is in the character's heart.

Candice's Spine

"Candice builds a community" could be the spine of her plot.

This is a shift from Candice searches for community, as it frames things differently. Rather than searching for it, she determines to build it. Each event moves her toward building that community, even when she fails. Those events make up the bones. The tendons are made from the goals that prompt each action, connecting each bone to the next. Combining both creates the spine.

Candice's Big Question

A big question for Candice's story could be this: Will Candice find her community? That big, overarching question would be established at the very beginning and not fully answered until the end. Each scene builds toward the answer. Smaller, related questions pull us through each chapter, building toward the answer to the big question at the end.

Using the Throughline, Spine, or Big Question

Any of these concepts could develop a plot, but each provides a different way to think about which events should link one to the other and culminate in a satisfying ending. By using any of these approaches —or a combination—the writer can analyze each scene and determine if it's part of the throughline, supports the spine, or moves toward answering the big question. This process can help determine if a scene belongs on the page.

Imagine that we write a scene about Candice fighting with a guy over a parking space. It could be funny and show her character, but if it doesn't relate in some way to Candice's motivation to find or build community, it should be cut or modified until it does.

Perhaps the guy she's fighting with sees the dog in her car and recognizes it, helping her find the owner. Perhaps the guy she's fighting with notices she's overly upset, and he stops arguing to ask if she's okay, allowing her to engage in an honest conversation with someone in her community. Maybe a third person watches the fight, breaks in on Candice's behalf, and shows Candice there are good people around and she can turn to them for support.

Any of those changes would modify the scene to make it fit into the throughline, become a part of the spine, or move toward the answer for the big question. Without something to link a scene to the throughline, spine, or big question, the scene goes on the chopping block, no matter how well written.

Why Middles are so Hard

There are several reasons why the middle is often the hardest to write: it requires fortitude to work through plot problems, pay attention to character development, and continue to raise the stakes.

It may seem odd that there is a much longer list of items required to have a successful beginning. But keep in mind that everything established in the beginning continues through the middle and culminates in the climax. Genre conventions continue. Character development, language use, description of location—all those aspects of the beginning must build and grow and be an active part of each scene throughout the middle and into the end.

The middle continues the threads created in the beginning and pushes the scenes toward the climax—that big event when the stakes are the highest and the obstacles are the biggest. The beginning must be solid enough to hold the middle up. Plus, each event must continue to build in terms of the obstacles and stakes.

The climax ends the middle and begins the end. We'll pick up with climax in the next chapter. For our next exercise, let's stay with the throughline, spine, and big question.

Exercise 4: Find the Throughline, Spine, and the Big Question.

Using any of these methods can help determine what drives a character through a manuscript. Define each of these for any work in progress or to build a new project.

Step One: Write one or two sentences to define the throughline, spine, and big question for a work in progress.

If there isn't a work in progress, invent a throughline, spine, and big question. That process will provide a tremendous amount of information to help finish, or even start, a first draft.

Step Two: Evaluate the strength of the throughline, spine, and big question. Ask the following questions: Is the throughline or spine strong enough to sustain an entire manuscript. Does the big question provide an important enough question to sustain the entire plot?

To help assess the strength, consider these examples.

"Candice seeks meaning in her life" is a strong throughline. "Candice seeks a job" is not.

"Candice finds her place in the world" is a strong spine. "Candice finds a job" is not.

"Will Candice find the dog's owner?" is not strong enough to hold up an entire novel, but "Will Candice find a way to live a contented life?" could pull Candice, and readers, through an entire manuscript.

The successful examples are more complex than the examples that fail. "Will Candice find a job?" would be a great question for a section of a novel, getting her closer to finding her community, but it's not enough to pull us through three hundred pages. For that, we need something with more depth, such as, "Will Candice survive grief and find meaning in life after a great tragedy?"

Short stories still need an important throughline, spine, or big question but obviously can focus on a smaller aspect of a character's life.

After writing and assessing all three, see which resonates. Choosing to work with one or more doesn't matter; what matters is that at least one provides guidance for building a plot. I do this for my own works in progress and tape the sentence or question to the edge of my computer monitor so I can refer to it while I work. These simple sentences can provide excellent guidance through the writing process, especially through the difficult middle, by keeping a focus on what drives a character, impacting their emotions and actions.

| 4 |

The End

> Leave 'em laughing or leave 'em crying, but mostly, just leave 'em.

All good things must come to an end, including a manuscript. The success of an ending can mean the difference between a book that people like and a book that people love. It can cause the reader to recommend the book to others or not. It can mean the difference between an agent offering representation or an agent passing. After working hard to hook and keep readers, don't let a poorly crafted ending ruin the project.

- Here are some ways to craft a successful ending:
- Complete a climax and provide a resolution.
- Answer the big question.
- Tie up (most) loose ends.
- Provide a question to keep readers imagining what's next.

Climax and Resolution

The climax bridges the middle and end of the project. It's the place near the end of the plot where the events become the most important. The objectives are the clearest for the reader and the characters, the obstacles are the biggest, and the stakes are the highest.

The climax may take more than one scene or chapter, so it can be useful to think of the climax in three parts as well, having its own beginning, middle, and end.

The beginning of the climax occurs when the protagonist confronts their biggest obstacle. It's the point where they admit what they truly want or face their biggest fear. It's the moment when the protagonist realizes that no matter how high the stakes, they are going to fight for their true goal.

The middle of the climax—as with the plot structure for the whole manuscript—contains the meat of the event. It's the biggest car chase, the declaration of love, the fight to the death. Filled with danger (physical, emotional, or psychological), the climax builds to the most important moment in the arc of the story.

At the end of the climax, the outcome becomes clear. Readers can see the way in which the character has been changed and at least a hint about how they might move forward in their life. Even if the character dies, that clarifies their future.

Two common constructions exist for the end of a plot regardless of whether the character achieves their super-objective or not. Those two constructs are resolution or resolution with a denouement.

When the big question is answered, the climax is complete, and the reader has a resolution. The reader understands the protagonist's potential future now that the biggest obstacle has been confronted. The tone of the resolution varies depending on whether the protagonist succeeds or fails in achieving their super-objective.

For a happy ending, the super-objective is not only attained, but the outcome is good. The lovers are together, the rancher saves the farm, the detective solves the crime. Or the super-objective turns out to be something entirely different than what the character expected, which the protagonist finally understands and accepts. For example, the lovers don't end up together, but each discovers that another person is their true love. The super-objective to find true love is attained, but not with the person that the character, and likely the reader, expected. The rancher loses the farm but moves to another piece of property that fulfills a different dream. The detective solves the crime but doesn't catch the killer.

For a sad or tragic ending, the obstacle might be too much of a challenge for the protagonist. The team loses the championship game, the mountain is too high to climb, the warrior dies before the end of the battle.

Another possible outcome is that the super-objective is achieved, but it isn't what the character needed or wanted. The climber reaches the top of the mountain but discovers it's not satisfying because in reaching the summit, they sacrificed a relationship, which they now realize meant more than scaling the peak. They are older and wiser, but not happier.

Sometimes characters get what they want, only to find out they pursued the wrong goal. For example, a lawyer fights to become a partner at the law firm, only to discover they would have been happier returning to their tiny hometown to take over their parent's solo practice.

If Ahab did kill the white whale in *Moby Dick*, but his ship sank and his crew was lost, did he achieve his goal? Melville left the issue of Moby Dick's survival unresolved because that's not the point of the novel. *Moby Dick* is not about whether the whale survives; it's about the fate of Ahab and his obsession. It's about Ishmael and his ability to overcome the troubles that sent him to sea. One of the lessons we learn from *Moby Dick* is that obsession can destroy a person and everyone around them, whether the original goal is achieved or not.

Resolution with a Denouement

Resolution with a denouement includes additional scenes after the resolution of the plot. Once the lovers end up together, the denouement would be any scenes of them living their new life. If the end of a plot shows a rancher heading out to buy a new piece of property, that is a resolution. If the end of the plot shows the rancher living on the new property, that is a resolution with a denouement.

Answer the Big Question

Scenes can be viewed as a series of smaller questions and answers leading up to the final climactic event. Just as the big question launches the plot at the beginning of the manuscript, the events of the plot answer the question at the end. Each scene, chapter, or section builds other, smaller questions that are asked and answered throughout, each pointing toward the big picture and the big question.

The big question must be answered, maybe with a yes and maybe with a no, but at least the outcome is understood. That process—answering the question—provides the resolution. Anything that occurs after the big question is answered can be a denouement.

Tie Up (Most) Loose Ends

While not every loose end has to be tied up at the end of the plot, readers will want most of them clearly resolved one way or another. There is some leeway for series authors to leave certain plotlines open, but the bulk of the questions set up for the reader must be answered by the final page. Each series book still needs to function as a standalone. Further, the writer makes a pact with the reader that important questions will be answered, so leaving too many open can feel unfair or sloppy.

If we return to Candice, think about what might be left open and what readers will expect to have answered.

If our big question for Candice is, "Can Candice find a community?" that question must be answered. One way to do that would be to have the plot resolve with her working for an animal rescue, living with the dog she saved, and content with the turns her life has taken.

That would be a happy ending, so what might we leave unanswered?

We could leave a question open about the potential for romance. For example, imagine if the final scene is Candice's romantic interest on their way over for dinner. We don't answer the question, "Will Candice find romance?" But we have left the door open that she might. If the big question of the book is, "Will Candice find romance?" not answering that question means we have failed to resolve the book in a satisfying way. If the big question is, "Can Candice find her place in the world?" and the answer to that is yes, then that outcome is good. We can leave the romance question open and still have a satisfying ending because the big question has been answered.

Keep in mind a resolution does not always mean characters get what they want. The plot is resolved if the ending answers the big question, not whether a character is happy. Answering the big question with the character's failure makes it a sad story, but still a successful plot.

Set Up a New Question

A potentially stronger choice than leaving a long-standing question unanswered can be to set up a new question. This can work whether the material is a stand-alone or a series.

A new question posed at the end of a manuscript can prompt readers to use their imaginations about what will happen next and how that question will be answered. For series authors, the new question can point toward the next book. This can be much more satisfying than leaving a question unanswered from early in the plot, which may feel like a letdown.

For example, if the question about Candice finding romance is only prompted at the end, readers are left with a solid question to play out in their own imaginations. One way to set that up would be that Candice doesn't look for romance throughout the plot. Maybe people she knows encourage it, but she dismisses romance as something she's not interested in or doesn't deserve. Then Candice finds her place in the world when she embraces her new job and her new dog, answering the big question: yes, she finds her place in the world. But in the final scene, the potential for romance arises, and the book asks the question, "Will Candice find romance?" Because it was prompted at the end, readers will be okay with having no resolution to that question because they get to decide for themselves if the romance blossoms. It's still satisfying because it wasn't asked early on.

Exercise 5: Assessing the Ending

Step One: Finding the Climax:

- Does the climax have a beginning, a middle, and an end?
- Does the super-objective become clear?
- Does the protagonist face their biggest obstacle?
- Are the stakes the highest?
- If not, what needs to happen in a rewrite to complete all three parts of the climax?

Step Two: Answering the Big Question

Copy the question from Exercise 3 and put it on the top of the page. Determine if that question is answered. If it is, there is a resolution. If it isn't, the manuscript may lack a clear, satisfying resolution. What work needs to be done to answer the big question? Use that information for an intentional rewrite.

Step Three: Tying up Loose Ends

What threads have been left untied? Confirm whether leaving those threads untied was intentional. If so, can it be justified? If there are too many, readers may feel cheated. It can be useful to write a scene where each thread is tied up, and after writing it, determine if the manuscript will be stronger with its inclusion.

Step Four: Identifying a New Question

What question does the end ask? If there isn't a new question at the end, determine a question and write a new ending based on that and see what happens. It will likely make for a stronger ending.

| 5 |

Stepping Through the Common Elements of Structure

> Know the rules, then decide whether to break them.

Though we have touched on some of the common elements of structure already, fully understanding each of these terms and having them all here in one place can help identify what's missing or needs work while assessing the foundation of a plot.

World Before

The World Before includes everything about a character's life at the beginning of a story. This ranges from their personal experiences to the location, era, and community. The World Before is the stasis in which a character exists before the intrusion of the inciting incident. Stasis means the character's life is unchanging; this is how they lived before the events of the plot.

A character exists in a context at the beginning. It could be a good, bad, or neutral situation. Then something changes in that situation to force the character to break out of their routine. If the character was in a good situation, the change could be dealing with a difference in fortunes. If the character was in a bad situation, it could be a shift to a strong and positive new context. If the character was going along without giving much thought to their life, their arc might deal with a realization that they already have a pretty good life, or that with some work, they can have a better life.

Change is hard for people, even if their life situation is bad, so any kind of upheaval creates stress and tension, even if it will ultimately be a change for the better.

Determining the characteristics of the World Before impacts the ultimate outcome of the manuscript. A character could change in many ways between their World Before and the end of the book. If the World Before is a good situation and the character ends up in a bad situation, that would make for a sad story. If the character is in a terrible situation in the World Before and ends up in a good situation, that would make for a happy story. If the character is in a terrific situation in the World Before, endures a tragedy, but ends up content at the end, that would be bittersweet.

Part of the character's—and by extension the reader's—emotional state at the end of the plot is determined by the context at the beginning.

Even writers working on memoir or narrative nonfiction have some degree of control based on how they frame events. A series of events could be viewed more positively or negatively in the outcome depending on the manner in which they are presented.

In a story where someone dies, a writer could present it as a tragedy by focusing on the loss of life. In contrast, the writer could focus on the joy and beauty that character experienced, and their death becomes not a tragedy, but a model of a life well-lived.

Writers must consider many questions when determining the character's World Before. Will readers hope the character returns to their old life? Arrives at a happier place? Do readers urge the character to succeed in a goal? Or recognize the character already has what they need and only lacks the ability to recognize their good fortune?

That scenario exists in every romance where the right person is in front of the protagonist the entire time but is overlooked as a romantic partner until the end.

The outcome—whether it's a happy ending or not—is determined in part by the degree of change between where the character starts and where they end up.

New World Order

At the end of the plot, characters achieve a new stasis. The manuscript ends with the protagonist (and often secondary characters) in a new normal that readers can imagine into the future. The juxtaposition between the World Before and the New World Order shows the extent of the character's arc. It's the context of their life before the series of events leading to the climax compared to the context of their life afterward.

Returning to Candice, her World Before was probably bleak and lonely. If we want her story to end happily, her New World Order is filled with friends, satisfying work, and the potential for romance. If we want the ending to be bittersweet, she might lose the dog somehow but come to understand she's finally open for love and companionship. Readers would feel sorrow that she didn't get to keep the dog she saved from the river, but also feel hope at the understanding that she has something to live for and the potential for happiness.

If we want to build a tragedy, she loses the dog and becomes overwhelmed, returning to the bridge.

Intrusion or Inciting Incident

The event that interrupts the World Before is often called an intrusion or an inciting incident. It is an action that impacts the protagonist and pushes them toward change. Think of it as the underlying event that launches the plot. Usually something out of the protagonist's control creates the intrusion, and the protagonist is pushed into action and must react.

Once the intrusion occurs, the protagonist drives the action, even if that means running from their super-objective for most of the plot. Curiosity about how the protagonist will deal with that inciting incident draws readers through the plot—and the subsequent events that spring from its intrusion.

One issue that can be confusing with regard to the intrusion is that it can occur prior to page one. A writer can drop readers in with a character already reacting to the intrusion, clarified later in the plot because the writer circles back to that event. Let's use Candice's story as an example.

In one version of the plot, Candice's emotional state in her World Before was that she was depressed and living alone in her small house not far from the river. She was in stasis, with nothing to either make her depression worse or give her reason to pull herself out. A letter arrived telling her that a friend has died. That letter was enough to put her over the edge and consider ending her own life.

That all happens prior to the start of the manuscript.

Chapter one begins the plot with Candice balanced on the bridge railing. She's ready to end it all, but saving the dog keeps her from jumping. She pulls the dog out of the river, then heads home to dry him off and track down the owner.

Finding the dog is not the intrusion, even though it may feel that way. But think about Candice's World Before. Her emotional World Before was not to be suicidal; it was depression. The event that incited her "change" from depressed to suicidal wasn't finding the dog; it was receiving the letter.

To show readers what the inciting incident was, we could have her return home, clean up the dog, call the local shelter, then notice the letter on the counter as she picks up her keys to leave. She could reread the letter, showing readers the contents. Or she could think to herself, *if it weren't for the dog, I would have committed suicide over this letter.* Or she could simply pick up the letter and throw it away, and we don't show readers the contents until a later scene when she discusses it with another person.

The point here is that the letter is the inciting incident that forces her to change her circumstances. Finding the dog is part of the plot after her life went from depression to suicidal. Chronologically, the intrusion (the letter) occurred before the plot starts, but readers don't know about it until later.

Keep in mind that linear and chronological are not always the same thing. The story is still linear. We see Candice ready to commit suicide because of something that occurred earlier in her life, but we don't learn what that was until later in the plot. In the chronology of events the inciting incident happens first. In the plot, which is linear, the earlier event isn't *revealed* to the reader until later.

Readers might not know what the inciting incident is at the beginning, but the character was impacted by the inciting event, which launches the plot. Readers are unlikely to think about the intrusion that launches a story, but they will feel the life of a character has been interrupted and hold their breath waiting to see if that will be good or bad.

How much of the World Before a writer establishes before the inciting incident is up to the writer, and, to some extent, dictated by genre. A thriller might drop readers into action at the beginning, with the inciting incident already in the past, whereas a coming-of-age story might have a longer section establishing the stasis of the character before showing the inciting incident in real time.

Writers would do well to have a sense of how the World Before is typically structured in their chosen genre. For example, a cozy mystery can have the murder victim show up fifty pages in, but a police procedural would do well to have a corpse appear in the first twenty, if not the opening pages, launching the investigation that propels the book.

What matters most is that the writer is aware of what launches each story and can draw a direct line through all the unfolding events back to that single event upon which everything else depends.

Rising Action

Rising action relates to events causing other events, which become more important each step of the way.

Whether writing a fictional story or writing about the real world, the layout of events works best if events become more important throughout a narrative, not less.

To build a foundation where events became less important would be like having the grand finale of a fireworks display at the beginning. Think of the letdown the audience would feel to have a tremendous explosion of light, sound, and color, and then spend the next twenty minutes watching the blasts die down to a trickle. The reason we like the grand finale at the end is because our excitement grows with each larger or more interesting boom.

With each detonation, the audience of a fireworks display wonders if it can be topped. A series of scenes function like a well-designed fireworks show, with each new round bigger or more complex. The finale—climax—is the culmination of the audience's expectations and the emotional release when it all comes together.

If pulling the dog out of the river was the most exciting event to happen in Candice's plot, readers would be disappointed by the manuscript.

Instead, each chapter both builds on the earlier events and surpasses them in terms of the level of importance to Candice. This is called rising action. The buildup of event (action) to event (reaction) causes the action to rise.

Climax

To reiterate, the climax is made up of three basic parts. The first part is when the protagonist reaches the moment where their objective is clearest, the obstacles are the biggest, and the stakes are the highest. It's that moment when readers hold their breath. Will the detective beat the killer in the fight? Will the lovers get together? Will the child reconcile with the parent? Those big, overarching questions are finally being faced.

To use Candice's story as an example, the first part of the climax might be that she is finally willing to take a chance and accept a friendship. This is just the beginning, so she has not yet overcome the biggest obstacle—accepting the friendship—but she is fully prepared to face it.

The second part is when the protagonist faces the biggest obstacle. For Candice, she could actively accept the friendship offered to her. That could mean making herself vulnerable in some way and taking a chance that another person will treat her well, and through that action finding her community.

The final part of the climax clarifies the way the character comes through the climax. Are they alive? Did they get what they wanted? Did they get what they needed?

If the protagonist overcomes the obstacle and the outcome is good, it's a happy ending. If they fail to overcome the obstacle and that's bad, it's a sad ending. If they overcome the obstacle, but that doesn't turn out to be a good thing, that could mark a tragedy. Or, if the obstacle isn't overcome, but that turns out to be okay, the ending could be bittersweet. Regardless of happy, sad, or poignant, the culmination leads to the resolution. With Candice, the end of the climax could be happy (a new friendship leading to community); bittersweet (a failed friendship, but the strength to try again); sad (a failed friendship and a descent into another depression); or tragic (a successful friendship that ends up becoming toxic or isolating).

Regardless of the protagonist's success, the outcome leads to a resolution.

Resolution

Resolutions are where readers understand the full scope of the character's arc. It's in these moments, as the climax fades, that we see who remains standing.

To return to the fireworks analogy, the climax starts when all the fireworks begin going off at once. We can feel, through the careful buildup of tension, that the biggest event is underway. Then the middle of the grand finale has the biggest explosions, but we feel the tide begin to shift the other way. We know an end is in sight, even if the biggest fireworks have yet to explode. Then the final big boom, followed by silence, shows the finale is over, and viewers know exactly how it ended—in a blaze of glory.

Let's create a full three-part climax for Candice, which might look something like this:

Beginning of the Climax: Candice realizes she's been holding back from connecting to the people in her community. She's faced with a decision to risk her physical well-being to help another person. Doing so will require her to be vulnerable emotionally as well as face physical danger.

Middle of the Climax: She commits to helping that individual, and the physical danger comes into play. Perhaps she has uncovered an illegal puppy mill, and she agrees to help an acquaintance gather evidence to take to the police and have the mill shut down. Candice puts her own safety and emotional state in the other person's hands.

End of the Climax: Candice and the other character establish a deeper relationship and successfully save the dogs in the puppy mill.

Resolution: Candice will move forward with a budding friendship and a new purpose in life: to save abused animals.

Denouement

A denouement is optional, based on how much the writer chooses to show of the New World Order. If the final scene ends with a hint toward the future, there is no denouement, and we end with the resolution. If, however, there is an epilogue or a chapter that establishes the New World Order, that is a denouement.

A denouement for Candice could be a chapter in which she and her new friend drive to another location where animals have been reported to be abandoned. Or if we have spiced the novel up with romance, she and the new friend could be drinking wine in front of the fireplace with whatever degree of sexual details are appropriate for the story—light romance, just a hint, erotica, full, graphic descriptions.

While there is no right or wrong about whether to include a denouement, it's more appropriate in some cases.

If a protagonist dies at the end, it would be tricky to show the New World Order unless the plot has integrated another character's point of view already or the plot is relayed by an omniscient or all-knowing narrator. Without either of those two scenarios, unless the protagonist experiences an afterlife, the story ends with their final breath.

With scenarios other than the death of the lone protagonist, a denouement could be appropriate. A romance might end with the lovers beginning their honeymoon. A sci-fi novel could end with the spaceship charting a course to a new location, and another planet comes into view. Series authors may want to use a denouement to hint at the next book. The phone rings in the private eye's office, and readers have a hint at what the next case will be.

Character Arc

Characters go on journeys through the course of a story. They start in one stasis and progress through the rising action, with events fundamentally changing them in some way. The New World Order comes from that experience. The change that comes from the difference between the World Before and the New World Order defines the character's arc. To stay with a character through an entire manuscript, especially a full-length one, and have them remain the same person they were at the beginning can feel unsatisfying for the reader. Regardless of whether a manuscript is fiction, true, or based on true events, readers want to see change in the people they read about.

Story Arc as Story Staircase

The story arc is determined by the plot. Another way to understand story arc is to think of it as a story staircase. A story rises in action from the opening to the climax, ending at a new "platform," which is the character's new stasis.

Imagine the World Before as a landing, the rising action as stairs, and the New World Order as the top platform. That's the same as the story arc but visualized another way. Readers experience the buildup to the climax, then the release at the resolution. Readers will have a release regardless of the outcome. Whether a story is sad, happy, hopeful, solemn, scary, violent, or peaceful, a solid resolution that ties up story threads provides a solid story arc.

Satisfaction doesn't come out of seeing a character achieve their goal. Satisfaction comes from seeing the attempt and the outcome. That's why readers can love a sad story or one in which the characters don't achieve their goals. For example, Shakespeare's *Macbeth* ends with almost everyone dead, yet audiences still love to watch the final scenes unfold. All the characters have big objectives, tackle huge obstacles, and face enormous stakes. The fact that so many of the characters fail doesn't change how successfully Shakespeare answered the big question and provided a solid story arc.

If any piece of a story arc is missing, the plot will feel unfinished. For example, if a step is missing out of the rising action, and readers aren't shown a pivotal event, that might stop them from finishing or lower the quality of their reading experience.

Imagine *Macbeth* if the audience never saw the witches, and Mac merely reported on them to his wife. Or if Shakespeare hadn't put Lady M on stage to stumble around trying to wash the blood from her hands. The final battle works in part because audiences see Mac face his enemies, and they realize right along with him that he has misunderstood the meaning of the fortunes the witches told him in an earlier scene. Viewers learn with him that he is not invincible, nor is he about to be a successful king.

If there is no climax, the reader can feel unfulfilled. They traveled the entire journey but didn't get the payoff. It would be like taking a hike to a mountaintop, then stopping before reaching the summit for no valid reason. Lastly, if there is no resolution, and too many threads are left untied, the reader can feel taken advantage of. After investing all their time to understand the character arc and watch events culminate in a big climactic scene, the writer cheats them out of understanding what it all meant.

Think about how a reader might feel if we didn't resolve Candice's relationship with the dog—he merely vanishes from the page. Or if it's unclear at the end if she's going to keep him. Those kinds of steps on Candice's staircase would need to be resolved to complete her story arc.

Understanding the roles of each of these common parts of a plot foundation can help identify flaws in a completed manuscript, locate holes in a work in progress, or determine what section to write for a new project. One way to tackle an unfinished draft is to identify which part is missing and write that missing piece before moving on to the next missing section.

Exercise 6: World Before and New World Order

One way to assess the success of a story and character arc is to compare the World Before with the New World Order.

Step One: Define the protagonist's World Before. Write a paragraph or make a list of bullet points. Include their physical, emotional, and psychological states.

Step Two: Define the protagonist's New World Order. Use the same format, either paragraph or bullet points. Then compare the two.

Step Three: Determine if the character (or characters if there is more than one protagonist) changes in a fundamental way. Do the character's circumstances change? If not, why not?

Determining why a character hasn't changed could provide important information for an intentional rewrite. Take the knowledge from this exercise and identify ways in which the character could demonstrate a new behavior or way of living their life. This will help ensure a solid character and story arc, both fundamental to a strong foundation.

For an unfinished manuscript or a new project, imagine the answer to these two questions and use that information to help push through to a complete first draft.

| 6 |

Building a Scene, Building a Chapter

> Scenes are building blocks for sections. Sections make up chapters. Chapters make up the whole.

Chapters are built by either a scene or a combination of scenes which connect to create a cohesive whole. Understanding how to define scenes can help writers build a stronger foundation, placing breaks in the best places to keep readers turning pages. Suspense and pace are controlled, in part, by where and how scenes begin and end. A scene can be determined by many factors, but one way I like to define a scene is through the parameters of time, place, and character action.

Time

Time plays a role in determining a scene. If an event unfolds in one continuous block of time, it can take place in one scene. If, however, an event takes place over multiple blocks of time, with time passing (off the page) in between, that event requires multiple scenes.

Any time the reader jumps forward or backward in time, a new scene starts.

Scenes have no requirements for length; the determinant is the un-broken nature of that time. Consider these examples.

If Candice's plot starts in the kitchen with her making breakfast, we might include a break in time, and the next event is Candice read-ing the letter informing her that her friend has died. Those are two different scenes. In contrast, we could create one long, unbroken scene in which Candice reads the letter, puts on her coat, and heads out the door. In the same scene we then describe everything she experiences on her walk. She arrives at the bridge, climbs up on the rail, see the dog, climbs down, and pulls him out of the water. That is one long, unbroken scene.

If we want to break that continuous event into multiple scenes, however, we can consider two other ways to break up scenes: location and character action.

Location

When characters shift from one location to another, that shift can also begin or end a scene. The exception to this is if the shift in loca-tion is continuous as in the scene described above, where we detailed Candice's entire journey to the bridge. Traveling in a plane, car, or train could be a single scene as well because the location changes outside the windows, but not inside with the character.

If Candice's location changes, but the description is unbroken, it could be a single scene. She could have breakfast, leave the house, and walk to the bridge, but if there isn't a break in time, the continuous change in location doesn't require a new scene.

If Candice's location changes with a break in description, it's a new scene.

She could have breakfast, then the next time readers see her, she's outside walking toward the bridge. This would be two scenes and could be indicated by a section break.

If the breakfast scene has a beginning, middle, and end, it could be a separate chapter. If not, this would become a chapter built of multiple scenes: the first at breakfast, then a section break, the next scene walking to the bridge, followed by another section break, and Candice after she arrives at the bridge.

Whether to make those scenes a single chapter or not would depend on whether each scene had a beginning, middle, and end, or if they needed to be combined for a chapter arc.

One last way to start and end a scene is through character action.

Character Action

Characters arriving or leaving a location or taking definitive action can also determine a scene, especially if the character's arrival or departure forces the characters already present to change their conversation or actions.

Imagine Candice at breakfast. She eats her toast and rereads her letter, and her emotional state goes from calm to agitated. She makes the decision to go to the bridge, slamming the door on the way out. The action (slamming the door) ends the scene. Even though the next scene might start on her doorstep with no break in time, her action changes the tone and can end the scene. Then we see her march down the road and travel to the bridge, which is a different scene from the one that took place in the kitchen, because her objective has changed. She now strives for a new goal.

Another example could be Candice at the bridge. One single scene could consist of her climbing the rail and preparing to jump. Readers would get a sense of what she's planning and wonder what she's going to do. Then readers discover the dog through Candice's eyes. Even though it's an animal, not a person, another character arrives in the scene. Her mood shifts as she sees the dog. Even before readers know she's going to step off the railing and save the dog, the shift in the tone ends the scene. She's gone from an internal conflict to an external conflict. She shifts from planning to end her life to focusing on helping the dog.

Here are two examples of how to end the scene by having the dog appear.

Candice stood balanced on the rail. The sun was warm on her neck, but a cool breeze rose from the dark water below. It would be simple to step off. Looking down, beyond her toes, something thrashed around in the water. A dog. The current pressed him against the concrete abutment. His head disappeared, and she held her breath until he appeared again.

He would never survive without her help.

In this example, establishing the potential that she will interact with the dog puts readers into a new scene. The objective of the previous scene was to end her life. But the arrival of the dog becomes an obstacle to that objective. If she jumps, the dog will also perish, which makes it a higher stakes obstacle for Candice. She will, of course, save the dog, thus launching the rest of the plot. But we could also set up the dog's arrival to end the scene with very little information. Consider the following:

Candice stood balanced on the rail. The sun was warm on her neck, but a cool breeze rose from the dark water below. It would be simple to step off. A sound, almost a cry, came from beneath her. Something thrashed around in the water.

It was a dog.

That's all it would take to end the scene. With the arrival of the dog, readers can guess that Candice is not going to kill herself; she's going to save the dog, but readers don't yet know how that will transpire. This creates tension for the reader.

By ending the scene, whether with the first or the second scenario, the reader's uncertainty about what happens next creates a question that draws the reader into the next scene.

She could jump anyway, and in the next scene we see her survive and end up with the dog, or she could get down off the rail, and in the next scene we see her save the dog. Both of these endings would generate the question, "Will the dog be saved?" And because of that action,

"Will Candice be saved?" Those strong questions will pull a reader into the next scene.

To review, three useful parameters exist to determine a scene: time, place, and character action. A scene can be continued or ended through a variety of combinations. If the POV character leaps forward in time, it's a new scene. If the POV character changes place, but not time, such as walking down a street or exiting a train, that could be a continued scene or the end of a scene, depending on the other parameters. If the POV character encounters new characters, causing a shift in the POV character's behavior in some way, that's likely a new scene. If the POV character continues with no other clear shift, it's likely the same scene.

Why It Matters

Scenes require a structure just as much as the full manuscript does. Scenes have a clear beginning, which sets up the event; a middle, which contains the bulk of the action; and an end, where the POV character changes parameters in some way. The shift could be in time, place, or through the arrival, departure, or action of a character, or any combination.

That shift, of time, place, or character action is where to put the chapter or section break. When done well, that shift creates a new question for the reader. If the scene doesn't have this type of structure, it may feel unnecessary, unfinished, or unsatisfying. This could also mean the reader stops reading.

Writers want readers to stay up all night, unable to put books down, and one of the most successful ways to create that need is through a question the reader needs answered. One of the ways to build a question is to end a scene with only the buildup to the answer, not the answer itself. This requires the reader to continue reading the next scene to know how it plays out. Then, after answering the question, the writer asks a new question, which then pulls the reader into the next scene.

If a scene ends without posing a question—Will Candice jump? Will the dog survive?—the reader may not care what happens next and close the book.

Before a manuscript can have a truly solid foundation, each individual scene requires a solid foundation. While a manuscript might move a character through a series of linked events, rising to a climax and reaching a resolution, if the individual scenes don't have structure, the manuscript can still fail.

Consider a house of cards. From a distance the structure looks okay, but a small wind will send the building tumbling.

As a developmental editor, I occasionally come across a manuscript that has character and story arcs, so the big picture works, but the individual scenes are poorly structured, providing information but without the foundation required for a solid manuscript. If multiple scenes don't create a question in the reader's mind or don't build up toward the next chapter or scene, an otherwise sound manuscript can fail.

Chapter Structure

Understanding scene structure helps with understanding chapter structure. Chapters can be a single scene or they may be several scenes linked together continuously or linked together with jumps in time and place and clarified through transitions.

In an example of a single-scene chapter, the entire chapter would take place within the parameters of time, place, and action. The chapter begins with a group of characters, which—for the most part—remain throughout the entire chapter. Secondary characters might arrive at the location or leave the location, but the time and action remains uninterrupted, and the POV character does not leave, thus keeping the parameters intact.

Consider this example. Candice stands on the railing considering whether to jump. Another character, Mack, strolls onto the bridge, curious about what Candice is doing. They have a conversation. This can remain a single scene, even though Mack wasn't there at the beginning. There's continuity of time and place, Candice remains the POV character, and her intention has not yet changed.

If Candice leaves the bridge and readers stay with Mack as the new POV character, that would start a new scene—and likely jar the reader with the shift away from our POV character.

Or Candice stands on the railing of the bridge, Mack arrives, and he says something that pulls her completely out of her thoughts about jumping. He could walk up and ask if she's seen a dog. She says no, hops down from the railing, and says, "But I'll help you look for him."

That breaks Candice's action, and potentially ends the scene.

The next scene could show Candice and Mack searching for the missing dog. That could be a new section in the chapter or a new chapter, depending on the length of the previous scene and the flow of the material.

The important part of this concept is that it is the shift in action that prompts a new scene, not just Mack's arrival at the location.

Whether to have a single scene or multiple scenes for a chapter is up to the writer. There is no right or wrong, just choice. A writer will want to identify the structure of all the chapters in a manuscript, however, and assess how they fit together. If most chapters are a single scene, one random chapter with multiple scenes could feel unbalanced or out of place. By the same token, if most chapters are built from multiple scenes, but one chapter consists of one long scene, that chapter may feel out of place. Either of these anomalies can be used to great effect, impacting the pace and tension if the choice is intentional and serves the plot. For example, maybe the climax is written in single-scene chapters for a faster pace and sense of urgency, in contrast with the multiple-scene chapters leading up to it.

Writing present tense lends itself to chapters with single scenes, with everything happening in real time. Past tense is more conducive to writing multiple scenes connected by transitions within a chapter, though single scenes can work in past tense as well.

For example, Candice arrives at the animal shelter with the dog she fished out of the river. The young woman at the counter recognizes the dog and leaves the front desk to go in the back. Candice remains at the counter, observing the activity at the shelter—dogs barking, workers playing with dogs in a yard, cars driving by outside. A moment later, a man comes through the door from the back of the shelter. He crosses over to the counter, looks down, sees the dog, and recognizes it as his own.

Even though the young woman at the counter has left and the dog's owner has appeared, the events are continuous from Candice's point of view. Candice remains at the counter of the shelter; her intention—to find the dog's owner—doesn't change, and there's no break in time. This could be an entire chapter.

Or we could build a chapter out of multiple scenes. Candice arrives with the dog, agonizing in the parking lot about whether to take him inside. That's a complete scene. A new scene places Candice inside with the dog, talking to the woman behind the counter. Then we break to a final scene where the dog's owner comes out from the back of the shelter and recognizes his dog. These three scenes could be an entire chapter.

Lastly, we could have a chapter for each of those scenes. An entire chapter could focus on Candice considering whether to go into the shelter. She might sit out front engaging with the dog, watching the people come and go. Maybe she gets on her phone to a friend. Then the next chapter takes her inside the shelter, where she has a long conversation with the woman behind the counter. Maybe she wants information about what will happen to the dog. Maybe she watches other people ahead of her in line. Then we have a third chapter when the dog's owner comes from the back of the shelter.

The choice to make this a continuous single scene or a chapter, a series of scenes, or even a series of chapters is up to us. Any of those scenarios would work, depending on what story we want to tell, the pace of the manuscript, and how much information we choose to include in each.

What matters most is that each chapter has its own beginning, middle, and end, and the end creates a question in the reader's mind that begs an answer, causing the reader to turn the page to read one more chapter, which then prompts another question.

Question-Answer-Question

One way to think about how to connect chapters is to use the pattern Question-Answer-Question.

Questions can be prompted for the reader without literal question marks at the end of the line. Let's take the three previous scenarios to illustrate what this might look like.

The first scenario shows Candice's visit to the shelter in one continuous scene. At the end of the scene, Candice reunites the dog with his owner. Let's call the dog Spanky.

The question that prompted us to keep reading after Candice arrived at the shelter was whether Candice would leave Spanky there. And what would become of the dog? The question about her leaving Spanky was answered, but we don't yet know the answer to what will become of the dog. How we write the reunion of the dog and Mack, the dog's owner, can answer the question of what will become of the dog. If Spanky is overjoyed at reuniting with Mack, readers know the dog will be fine. If Spanky is terrified of Mack, readers know the dog will not be fine. If Spanky is torn between Candice and Mack, readers don't know if the dog will be fine.

How we end the scene can prompt the next question.

If Spanky is thrilled at reuniting with Mack, and Mack and Candice hit it off, the new question might be, "Will Candice and Mack form a relationship?" Or "Will Candice get another dog now that she sees how happy Mack and Spanky are to be reunited?"

If Spanky is terrified at reuniting with Mack, the new question might be whether Candice will steal Spanky back, or if she will find another way to save him from Mack.

If the dog is torn between Candice and Mack, we've created the question of who will ultimately get the dog. Or will Mack and Candice form a relationship and share him?

Overlapping questions show how the same story can be approached in different ways. In this early draft stage, perhaps we know we want Mack and Candice to get together by the end, but we want them to fight over the dog first, with the dog as the catalyst for their romance.

Regardless of what we choose, our final paragraph or line of each chapter will create a question in the readers' minds that makes them turn the page to find the answer.

Multiple questions can be asked throughout a chapter, whether it's one continuous scene or multiple scenes. Will Candice go inside with Spanky? Will the woman at the counter help? Who is she going to get from the back of the shelter? Who is Mack? How does Spanky respond to him? Each of those are asked and answered in the chapter itself; then either a new question is asked at the end, or an old question is reiterated for the reader to remember that something still needs to be discovered.

For the example with three separate chapters, the following questions take us from chapter to chapter: Will Candice go inside the shelter? Will the woman at the counter help? Who is Mack? What does Spanky think about reuniting with his owner? Then finally, where does this leave Candice?

But don't forget the big question we generated for Candice's plot: Will Candice find a community?

If that is the big question drawing Candice—and readers—through this plot, then each of these scenes, and the questions they generate, connect to that in some way.

We could make that happen in lots of ways.

Maybe Candice decides to volunteer at the shelter, and she discovers her love of animals and a natural talent with training dogs.

Maybe Candice falls for Mack, and their romance takes her life in a new direction with a new group of people.

Maybe Candice determines Mack is a terrible dog owner, and she dedicates the entire plot of the novel to stealing the dog back, finding allies along the way who become her community.

Any of those could connect these scenes to the big question.

What wouldn't work very well would be if Candice drops Spanky at the shelter, Mack appears to be a good dog owner, Spanky is happy to see him, Candice leaves, and no mention is ever made of Spanky or Mack again.

That would feel like an unrelated event that doesn't move the plot forward, no matter how well it's written.

We could use this as a device to pull Candice out of her sorrow. She goes home and continues her life, never to consider suicide again, but each event functions best if it causes a change in a character, for better or worse, pushing them in the new direction prompted by the inciting incident. It will be infinitely more satisfying if the event with Spanky sends Candice in a new direction—one she wouldn't have taken otherwise.

The plot for Candice's story will have a much stronger structure if her interaction with Spanky clearly reshapes her life, sending her down a new road that wasn't clear or available to her before she met the dog.

Link Upon Link

Another way to think about how chapters relate to each other is to imagine links in a chain. Each step on Candice's journey—finding Spanky, taking him to the shelter, meeting Mack, and returning the dog to his owner—is linked by a common thread. The common thread here is Spanky, but it can also be Candice thinking of something other than her own immediate troubles, or Candice on the path to discovering true love, or Candice finding her true passion.

Even if we mixed chapters from different POV characters into the manuscript, if Candice is our protagonist, we will return to her storyline, and her scenes will link, regardless of other scenes occurring in between. And most likely, the other POV characters relate in some way to Candice's story, either as a parallel subplot or characters in Candice's sphere who will participate by either helping or hindering Candice from finding her community.

Exercise 7: The Structure in Scenes and Chapters

It's useful to analyze a manuscript's structure scene by scene and chapter by chapter. Starting at page one, identify each scene based on the parameters of time, place, and character action. Check for the following:

- Is each chapter a single scene or broken into multiple scenes?
- Is this consistent from chapter to chapter, or does it vary?
- Why do the chapters vary? Is that an intentional choice or by accident? Is there a pattern or is it random?
- If pace is an issue, varying chapter construction could be the problem. Check if there are long chapters with multiple scenes that have no arc. That could bog material down. Or, if every chapter is a single scene, perhaps there is no break for the reader and everything is rushed. For many genres, that might be too fast. Or, if the chapters are a chaotic mix where some are multiple scenes and others are single scenes, the pace could feel uneven. Try adjusting the location of chapter breaks to create consistency in chapter construction. Check that each chapter has a beginning, middle, and end, with the end launching the reader into the beginning of the next chapter.
- Does each individual scene have an arc? If not, what's missing? Rewrite to provide an arc to each scene.
- Does each chapter end with a question to prompt the reader to continue reading? This doesn't have to be a literal question. Think of it as a final line or paragraph that produces a question in the reader's mind.

It's a long, slow process to work through an entire manuscript, chapter by chapter, scene by scene, but this can solve a host of problems with a completed draft that isn't working. For those with a partial draft, use this exercise to help finish a first draft. Consider each scene and chapter, find the arcs, find the question at the end, and let the answer to that question lead toward the next event.

For anyone working on a first draft of something new, use this exercise to write through to the end or create an outline.

Still struggling? Read on for some tips on getting through a first draft along with other common problems.

| 7 |

Failure to Finish a First Draft and Other Common Problems

> All stories begin with a single scene. Write one, and the rest will follow. Until they don't.

Understanding the structure of scenes and how they work together, the structure of a chapter, and the arc of a full plot will make a writer's work stronger. These concepts are not just for fiction; they are applicable to memoir and narrative nonfiction as well. But understanding foundation doesn't help if a writer can't get a scene down on the page or only manages to string a few chapters together, then runs out of steam. Let's take a look at the struggle to finish a first draft, then look at some common foundational issues in fiction, memoir, and narrative nonfiction.

Unable to Finish a First Draft

One issue can be writing like gangbusters for a few chapters only to have the story go flat. The writer gets stuck, unable to reach a conclusion.

Often, the problem is that the writer doesn't know what the book is about.

This can also be true for narrative nonfiction and memoir. Even when writing about true events, the content needs a purpose.

Take memoir. I could write about being an author or about being a developmental editor or being a professor or being a playwright and theater artist. Any single one of those could work for a memoir. But if I wrote about all of them, it would be sprawling and unfocused. Choose one, and I would have a clear, concise purpose.

With regard to narrative nonfiction, let's use the 2022 Olympics. Writing narrative nonfiction about the Olympics would be an enormous project. No writer could cover every event, every athlete's personal story, and all the actions throughout the games. But we could write only about the Russian skater accused of using performance enhancing drugs or about how that event impacted the other skaters.

Either of those stories could be a tight focus on only one aspect of the Olympics, not the entire event, the city, the country, and every single person involved with the games.

Knowing where the protagonist (whether a real person or fictional) is headed can often solve the problem of finishing a first draft because it will crystalize what the overall story is about.

My advice in this situation is to write the ending. Using the creative child, write an ending that makes sense based on what the writer knows about the "given circumstances" of the protagonist. Is it a happy ending or a sad one? Does the character get what they want or not? What does the character learn? In what direction do the opening scenes send the character, and what is a likely outcome based on that inciting incident?

It doesn't matter if the ending changes during a later draft or becomes an earlier scene or is cut altogether. What helps is having a direction to write toward.

Get the first draft done.

Writing is like going on a road trip. Whether sorting out an outline or discovering the events of a manuscript on the page, it can be useful to know where to start and where to end.

Consider the following: A driver leaves Los Angeles on Interstate 10, travels up Highway 177, then takes Highway 62, doubling back west. The driver left LA at ninety miles an hour, racing along under bright blue skies and hearing the call of the road. The first turnoff is still exciting, the landscape new, the driver's blood pumping to the music on the radio. But by the time the car arrives in Joshua Tree, the driver realizes they haven't even left California yet. Disappointed, they pull over, stop at a gas station for bad coffee and a bag of peanut M&Ms, and the trip comes to an abrupt and unsatisfying halt.

Think how different it would be if the driver left Los Angeles, knowing their ultimate destination is Boston. Racing out of the city on Interstate 10, the driver veers at the last minute onto Interstate 15, then heads north and hits Interstate 40 at Barstow. Stay on 15? Or take 40? Either road will get the driver closer to Boston. A quick decision: take Interstate 40 to Albuquerque, where another decision will be made.

Compare this to the writing process. In the first instance, the writer has an idea for a story. It might even be a great idea, worthy of a full-length manuscript. The opening scenes come easy, playing out in the mind like a movie. Then the idea starts to falter, the writer unclear on the point of it all. Stumbling to a halt, the writer throws up their hands and says, "I can't see where to go next. I'm sure the concept is the problem, it's not good enough, that's okay, I have others."

Then the writer repeats the same process all over again with a new idea, never finishing a first draft. That may be because the concept isn't the problem; a weak foundation is the problem.

This could play out in a different way. The writer has an idea for a story. The opening scenes come easy, playing out in the mind like a movie. *Before* the idea begins to falter, the writer moves to the end, writing out the final or climactic scenes.

Without losing energy, the writer returns to the opening chapters knowing where the action will lead. Each event builds on the previous, with a specific, clear goal in mind—to reach that final scene. It doesn't matter if the writer creates scenes out of order, or writes an outline, building from the beginning to the end, as long as the writer develops a full first draft.

Either way, using the foundation, knowing that the opening scenes lead toward a specific end, knowing the events will become more important, and knowing that each scene will lead—like a series of step-ping-stones—to the final moment that is already written, the writer never gets lost along the way.

This may help a writer struggling to finish a first draft, but there are also a few common problems for authors who have a draft but don't know what to do next. These include flat structure, events on the page, and events off the page.

Flat Structure in a First (or Subsequent) Draft

A common problem in drafts that don't quite work is a lack of rising action. If each scene carries the same weight as the one before, there's no buildup toward a climax. One way to assess this is to read each scene or chapter and identify the stakes. Do the stakes become higher as the plot progresses? Is the character in more danger emotionally, physically, or psychologically? How invested is the protagonist in their super-objective? While those are character questions, writers can solve that problem through foundation. Identify places where the stakes don't rise. How can the writer raise them? What can the writer do to the character to make the flat line of scenes turn into a staircase?

Identify whether the scenes build on the previous scenes. If they don't, that points to a structural problem. Determine what scenes are unnecessary for the plot and what scenes are missing. Cut anything that doesn't relate, or rewrite the scene so it builds on what happened before.

If the scenes build on each other but there's no rise, great—just raise the stakes. Make the outcome of the events more important. One way to do this is to keep the character from getting what they want for a longer period of time. Throw more obstacles in their path. If it's fiction, that's where the creative child comes in. Let your creative child imagine scenarios—nothing is too outlandish while building a solid draft with rising action. The critical eye can always be employed later to identify anything that's not appropriate for the genre or style of the work.

Events off the Page

Regardless of genre or whether a work is fiction or nonfiction, another common problem occurs when the writer leaves the best parts off the page.

Writers are sometimes their own worst readers. What is glaringly obvious to an outside reader can be difficult for a writer to identify. Part of this is because a writer knows the entire story and may not realize some of the important scenes have not made it to the page.

Sometimes a writer balks at writing the tough stuff. It can be hard to put a beloved character in danger. It can be challenging to write honestly about difficult aspects of our own lives and share the worst events from our past. Further, it can be easy to lose the trees for the forest. By this I mean the writer may have a handle on the larger manuscript—there's a beginning, a middle, and an end—but the writer doesn't look closely at each individual scene to identify if something is missing.

This issue can be addressed in multiple ways. One is to walk away from the manuscript for a period of time. At least a week. Maybe a month. Then come back and read a hard copy. The time away, as well as reading on the page rather than the screen, can help the writer remove themselves from the process. It allows the writer to read as if it is someone else's story. This can make it much easier to identify missing scenes or places where the reader needs the character to face bigger obstacles.

Another practice that can help is to sl-o-o-o-w down. I can't emphasize this enough. One of the biggest obstacles for writers is that writing is a marathon, not a sprint. Rushing through rewrites can cause a writer to miss all kinds of important issues including missing scenes or keeping scenes that don't matter. Slow the process down.

Read slowly.

Read paragraphs slowly.

Read chapters slowly.

Then read them again.

Be honest. Are all the important scenes fully fleshed out on the page? Or are some missing or glossed over? Slowing down can work wonders for the quality of a writer's work. Slowing down can eventually speed up the overall process because writers fix problems the first time through rather than doing multiple quick read-throughs.

Lastly, having a trusted beta reader can help identify missing sections. I have a few suggestions for working with a beta reader. One is to have a reader who reads in the same genre. While people can critique manuscripts in genres they don't typically read, it can be extremely useful to have a reader versed in the conventions of a genre or age range. Second, keep in mind the reader has only one opinion. Pay attention to their feedback but trust internal instincts for what needs to change. A writer should never apply feedback they disagree with or don't understand. Having said that, often the comments that rankle the most are the ones to pay the most attention to. It's hard to hear our baby is ugly, but better to hear it from a beta reader than twenty agents or twenty reviewers.

Finally, it can be very helpful for the beta reader if the writer asks specific questions of them, such as, "Are there holes in the plot or scenes missing from the page?"

When I work with beta readers, I usually provide a few specifics I am wondering about, and end with "or anything else that stands out to you." This allows the beta reader to know what I'm concerned about but encourages the freedom to add in observations about issues I may not be aware of or haven't thought of.

Too Many Events on the Page

Much like the issue of events happening off the page that readers should see, unnecessary scenes on the page can cause a manuscript to fail. As I've said before, scenes build on each other and connect, but there can be what my granny called "too much of a good thing." Writers can make the mistake of showing ten scenes about something when one would do.

Applying the same techniques as recommended for Events off the Page, a writer can let material sit for a while, then read a hard copy, read slowly, and engage a beta reader. The question for the writer or beta reader might be, "Are there any places where the reader finds the work repetitive or redundant?"

Those would be places to cut or combine into single scenes.

Common Problem for Memoir

Keep in mind that memoir functions with many of the conventions of fiction and is pitched the same way—with a complete, polished, and engaging manuscript. Identify the personal super-objective of the memoir. What is the single driving goal that gives the memoir shape? Stringing together scenes from a person's life doesn't make a plot, and memoir still requires plot. Plot in memoir also requires a throughline, with objectives, obstacles, and stakes, combined with action.

Make sure the super-objective is important enough to carry a full-length manuscript with the events rising in intensity of action and stakes. The super-objective must be important enough to write about for a couple hundred pages, and the author must overcome obstacles with big stakes; otherwise, what is the point of the memoir?

Use the same techniques to build suspense and rising action for the scenes. Just as with fiction, the scenes work best if they build on each other. No matter how interesting side events in the author's life may be, they are unlikely to pull a reader through if they aren't connected to the throughline. A memoir needs a spine, scene structure, and chapter structure just like fiction. The author is the character, and a specific aspect of their life is the story arc.

One of the most common issues I see with memoir is a lack of structure, with unrelated scenes strung together rather than a clear throughline. A memoir is not an autobiography. It's not a chronological telling of a person's entire life. It is a dramatic retelling of a specific event or series of connected events. It may cover a lot of years. It may include a lot of different events, but a skeleton functions underneath all that, with each vertebra (event) connected to the next with tendons (objectives). Examples of memoir topics might include dysfunction in a family, which the author overcomes; addressing a personal problem, even if it takes forty years to do so; or surviving grief. Regardless of the topic, each scene in a memoir relates to a specific aspect of the author's life. Other aspects won't come into play.

Narrative Nonfiction

Narrative nonfiction can have the same problems as memoir. The writer has one specific story to tell, even if multiple primary characters are involved in a complicated series of events. Underneath it all lies a clear throughline, scene to scene. Or a clear spine—person connected to person. Or a big question that ties scenes together. With extraneous scenes in memoir or narrative nonfiction, the author risks losing readers' attention, just as they would with fiction.

Exercise 8: Finish the Draft/Assess the Draft

As I've included suggestions for working with a flat draft or a draft with missing or too many scenes, this exercise is geared toward those trying to finish a first draft or to assess a draft.

As described earlier in this chapter, it's advisable to encourage the creative child to write the ending. This releases the unfettered imagination and creates a final stop on the journey, providing something to write toward. But sometimes that fails. That's when the grownup—the critical eye—comes into play.

It's time to force an ending.

Step One: Require the critical eye to come up with a plausible scenario for the story arc. Use the following formula to discover an ending. Fill in the blanks with the names and events for the work in progress.

(Name) gets into trouble when (this happens).

Then (this happens).

Then (this happens).

Repeat then this happens (with new events) until the basic plot is outlined.

Culminating when (this happens).

Resulting in (this).

Use the critical eye as a taskmaster, not an editor. Don't assess the quality of the writing; just get the content down.

Step Two: Write a final scene using the information from Step One.

Step Three: Go back to the beginning of the manuscript and let the final scene pull the writing through to the end. Use the final scene as a guide for finishing the first draft. Edit later. Just get the words down for a beginning, middle, and end.

To Assess a Draft:

Step One: Use Step One as outlined above to identify the big events of the plot. This is the simplest method of identifying a basic beginning, middle, and end.

Step Two: Check that the current final scene fits the outline from Step One. If not, rewrite.

Step Three: Let the outline from Step One guide a read-through to confirm there's a direct line between big events and the climax. Make notes where events don't fit or aren't resolved, then use that information to direct a rewrite.

| 8 |

Final Thoughts

> Without a solid foundation, the best written sentences won't matter, and even the most fascinating characters or premise will fail to hold a reader's interest.

Structure is one of the most important aspects of craft for a writer to master. Let's review four pivotal concepts for building a strong foundation.

- Character is built from action.
- Action builds plot.
- Plot rises to a climax.
- The climax answers the big question asked at the beginning.

If any of those aspects are missing, the manuscript will likely fall like a pile of Jenga blocks with too many supports missing. Each of these four aspects of foundation are key to a successful manuscript.

Characters are Built from Action

Characters are a combination of what they say, think, and do. Readers know what each of the characters say and do, but with one exception, they only have access to what the POV character thinks—don't make the mistake of popping into the thoughts of other characters, unless writing from an omniscient point of view—though there is still only one POV, that of the omniscient voice or narrator.

An omniscient point of view distances the characters from the reader. Don't confuse POV with protagonist here. While the omniscient narrator, who functions as the POV character, can have access to all the characters' thoughts, one character still remains central. Further, "head-hopping," the term applied to intrusively popping in and out of different characters' points of view, can still arise in omniscient writing if the omniscient narrator is too close to multiple characters' internal experiences. Omniscient is not necessarily intimate. It is the distance from the characters that allows for omniscient point of view.

But what characters say carries less weight than what they do. Action is the primary component for a reader to understand character.

Action Builds Plot

Characters act, doing something that impacts their lives and the lives of those around them. This provokes a reaction, moving the plot forward. Action connected to action builds plot. Actions are events which build on each other, rising in importance throughout the story to reach a climax.

Plot Rises to a Climax

Events build to a climax, when the super-objective is the clearest, the obstacles are the biggest, and the stakes are the highest. Throughout the climactic event or series of events, the reader will understand if the protagonist achieves their biggest goal and whether that outcome is positive or negative. This resolution of the plot determines if the story is sad, happy, tragic, or bittersweet.

The Climax Answers the Big Question

Plots evoke a big question at the beginning—a question that draws readers through the book. Will the protagonist find love? Will the underdog win the fight? Will Candice find her community?

This big question results in many smaller questions that are asked and answered throughout the chapters, culminating in an answer to the big question during the resolution of the climax.

Think of these four concepts as key identifiers for assessing the underlying foundation of a plot. If those key identifiers aren't there, go back through this guide and walk through each exercise, identifying where the foundation requires more work.

The good news is that structure can be learned and applied to any writing project. By using this guide, I hope each writer can identify issues in their own writing and rewrite their manuscript into a query-ready project. Use this guide throughout the writing process, dipping back into the sections and exercises that most resonate for any specific issue.

Final Exercise

Having a more complete understanding of structure, it's time to do a final intentional rewrite for foundation. I highly recommend doing all the previous exercises before tackling this one.

Let the work in progress sit for at least two weeks, though a month would be even better. It's hard to step away, but take that time to work on other projects. Have a vacation or a staycation. Work on social media. Take advantage of a self-imposed break.

After the break, do the following:

Step One: Print the entire manuscript and read it in one single, uninterrupted sitting.

This will likely take all day, so keep the following in mind before starting.

First, work uninterrupted. If uninterrupted time is unlikely because of others in the house, get a hotel room, go to a friend's house, head to the library, or if the weather is nice, go to the park. If it's impossible to carve out quiet space, at least let everyone in the house know there are to be no interruptions for any reason for a full day. For those writers with young children, this could be a great time to invest in a babysitter, reach out to family for help, or break this exercise into chunks. Some writers may not be able to take uninterrupted writing time. When breaking this into chunks, try not to let a whole day pass in between sections—make the session days back-to-back.

Obviously, take breaks for food and a stretch, but keep those breaks limited and don't engage in conversations or anything that will pull focus from the work. Turn the phone off, or allow for only specific phone numbers, such as the babysitter, to come through in case of emergency. Avoid talking to anyone or watching television or reading. Keep focus on the work in progress.

Reading the entire manuscript in one sitting provides an excellent overview of the foundation. Don't use this read-through to fix issues on the page; that could take a lot longer than a day. Read a hard copy as much like an outside reader as possible. Don't fix anything. Just take notes on the page.

Step Two: After completing the uninterrupted read-through, take a break of as much time as needed—days, weeks, a month—then go back to address each note. This can take several days, if not more, depending on how many issues the writer identifies and the speed of rewriting.

Once every note has been resolved, the manuscript likely has a solid foundation. Time to read through again and repeat the process until reading the material in one sitting results in no additional notes.

Just starting a new project? Great! In that case, the final exercise is to write a first draft of that new project. Then go back through this guide as many times as necessary, applying the information to the first draft and subsequent drafts until the entire manuscript can be read through without making a single change or note.

Congratulations on reaching the end of this guide!

But don't forget, even applying each of these concepts is not a guarantee that the manuscript is query ready. Use the other books in this series to help with additional issues such as poor character development, awkward dialogue, and unpolished drafts. It's also possible that a professional outside eye is the next best step. Feel free to reach out to me and the rest of the editors at Allegory Editing for more information. From developmental editing to copy editing and proofreading, it has become more and more important that writers utilize all the opportunities available to produce the most polished manuscript possible before beginning the query process.

My super-objective is to make your writing goals come true, so don't miss any of the guides in my Wait, Wait, Don't Query (Yet!) Series.

Elena Hartwell has spent years supporting writers and constructing stories. Her award-winning and best-selling works include the Eddie Shoes mysteries and *All We Buried* (written under Elena Taylor). Her plays have been seen around the US and UK, garnering critical acclaim and stellar reviews. As a developmental editor she has worked with hundreds of writers, most recently as senior editor and director of programming for the boutique editing house, Allegory Editing. She regularly teaches writing workshops and enjoys helping others achieve their writing dreams.

To learn more about Elena, visit www.ElenaHartwell.com

Photo by Mark Perlstein

ACKNOWLEDGMENTS

It takes a village to turn a manuscript into a book. I could not have done this without my community.

Much gratitude to Christine Pinto for solid feedback and constructive criticism. This project would be a hot mess without her help. To Andrea Karin Nelson, for both feedback on the manuscript and building a home for me at Allegory Editing. It's a constant reassurance to know she has my back. Tremendous appreciation to Amy Cecil Holm, whose sharp eyes and attention to detail turned my final draft into a polished book. A very special thanks to OnTheBrinkDesigns for the cover art and web design. To Sheila Sobel, my comrade in arms, for her beta reading and unwavering support. To my hubby JD Hammerly, who makes so much possible. And to my favorite beta reader of all time, my mom Sherry Hartwell—you have always been my rock.

www.ingramcontent.com/pod-product-compliance
Lightning Source LLC
Chambersburg PA
CBHW060253030426
42335CB00014B/1676